IMPROVING

THE PERFORMANCE

OF GOVERNMENT

EMPLOYEES

A Manager's Guide

Stewart Liff

AMACOM

American Management Association

New York • Atlanta • Brussels • Chicago • Mexico City • San Francisco
Shanghai • Tokyo • Toronto • Washington, D.C.

Bulk discounts available. For details visit:
www.amacombooks.org/go/specialsales
Or contact special sales:
Phone: 800-250-5308
Email: specialsls@amanet.org
View all the AMACOM titles at: www.amacombooks.org

This publication is designed to provide accurate and authoritative
information in regard to the subject matter covered. It is sold with
the understanding that the publisher is not engaged in rendering
legal, accounting, or other professional service. If legal advice or other
expert assistance is required, the services of a competent professional
person should be sought.

Library of Congress Cataloging-in-Publication Data

Liff, Stewart.
    Improving the performance of government employees : a manager's guide
/ Stewart Liff.—1st ed.
        p.   cm.
    Includes index.
    ISBN-13: 978-0-8144-1622-8
    ISBN-10: 0-8144-1622-5
    1. Performance.   2. Employee motivation.   3. Responsibility.   4. Civil
service—Personnel management.   I. Title.
HF5549.5.P35L54   2011
352.6'6—dc22
                                                            2010031666

About AMA

American Management Association (www.amanet.org) is a world leader in talent
development, advancing the skills of individuals to drive business success. Our mission
is to support the goals of individuals and organizations through a complete range of
products and services, including classroom and virtual seminars, webcasts, webinars,
podcasts, conferences, corporate and government solutions, business books and research.
AMA's approach to improving performance combines experiential learning—learning
through doing—with opportunities for ongoing professional growth at every step of one's
career journey.

Printing number

10   9   8   7   6   5   4   3   2   1

This book is dedicated to my mother, Pearl, and my father, Hal. No child ever had a better set of parents.

Contents

Acknowledgments

So many people were involved in helping me write this book that it is impossible to acknowledge everyone. However, I'd like to start off by thanking my editor, Christina Parisi, for her assistance and for the confidence she has shown in me. She has always been a great support to me on the different projects we have worked on. I would also like to thank Jim Bessent, Associate Editor with AMACOM. Jim has been a pleasure to work with.

As always, I'd like to acknowledge my four primary mentors, Joe Thompson, Tom Lastowka, Bill Snyder, and Paul Gustavson, as well the many other people who have mentored me over the years, including but not limited to Pat McLagan, Peggy Hutcheson, Ann Hermann-Nehdi, Paul Draper, Alan Checketts, Rick Nappi, Barry Jackson, Herman Greenspan, Dan Kowalski, Dan Bisgrove, John Coghlan, Dave Walls, and Montgomery Watson.

A special thanks as well to Pamela A. Posey, D.B.A., for everything she has taught me over the years. I would also like to recognize Michelle Clark for her tireless advice and support and Jodie Mendelson for the drawings that she has contributed to this book.

To my government friends Dennis Kuewa, Gloria Young, Grant Singleton, Pat Amberg-Blyskal, Ed Russell, Lynda Russell, Susan Fishbein, Bob Dolan, Ben Weisbroth, Paul Koons,

Ken Clark, Michele Kwok, Veronica Wales, Mike Harris, Julius Williams, Dorothy MacKay, Debbi Greitzer, Bob Epley, Steve Simmons, Jenn Kler, Ray Jefferson, and many others I did not mention, I want you all to know I appreciate your service to this country and am honored to have you as a part of my life.

I would never have been able to write this book without the loving support of my family. As always, a deep, heartfelt hug to Jaffa Schlusselberg; my father-in-law, Herman; my brother, Jeff; my three wonderful children, Rob, Jen, and Marc; my nephew, Matt; and my stepchildren, Rob and Amy. Also, I want to thank Matt's cats, Penny, Twix, Colby, and Frisky, who provided me with great comfort during the most difficult time of my life.

Finally, I want to thank my best friend in life—my wife Lisa. She was with me every step of the way as I wrote this book.

Stewart Liff
Santa Clarita, California

PART 1

Systems Thinking

Overview

The Government Performance and Results Act (GPRA)

In recognition of the growing concern regarding the perform-ance of the federal government, in 1993 Congress enacted the Government Performance and Results Act (GPRA).[1] This legis-lation changed the way that the federal government managed its performance by requiring federal agencies to become results-oriented. "The Government Accountability Office (GAO) has described GPRA as being 'the centerpiece of a statu-tory framework Congress put in place during the 1990s to ad-dress long-standing weaknesses in federal operations, improve federal management practices, and provide greater accountabil-ity for achieving results.'"[2]

Its goals were to:

> "(1) improve the confidence of the American people in the capability of the Federal Government, by systemati-cally holding Federal agencies accountable for achiev-ing program results;

(2) initiate program performance reform with a series of pilot projects in setting program goals, measuring program performance against those goals, and reporting publicly on their progress;

(3) improve Federal program effectiveness and public accountability by promoting a new focus on results, service quality, and customer satisfaction;

(4) help Federal managers improve service delivery, by requiring that they plan for meeting program objectives and by providing them with information about program results and service quality;

(5) improve congressional decision-making by providing more objective information on achieving statutory objectives, and on the relative effectiveness and efficiency of Federal programs and spending; and

(6) improve internal management of the Federal Government."[3]

The Act required agencies to develop long-term strategic plans that identified outcome-related goals and objectives, explained how the goals and objectives would be achieved, identified the key external factors to the organization and beyond its control that could hamper its achievement of the general goals and objectives, and explained the program evaluations used in developing or adjusting the general goals and objectives, with a timetable for future program evaluations.

Each agency was further required to prepare an annual performance plan for every program activity contained in its budget. The plan had to establish performance goals defining the level of performance to be achieved by an activity; list such goals in a quantifiable and measurable form, if possible; describe what was required to meet these goals; develop the appropriate performance indicators; and provide a way to compare program results with the established performance goals.

The GPRA is important to this discussion because it changed the focus of federal agencies from process/compliance to outcomes. It let everyone know that, more than ever, they would be accountable for achieving the desired results. This important distinction placed that much more pressure on government managers at all levels to deliver excellent performance.

Why Is It So Difficult to Manage Performance in the Government?

The simple reason it is difficult to manage performance in government is that there are a wide variety of factors and variables at play, a number of which are extremely difficult to manage and control. By the same token, it is important to recognize that many of these factors and variables are not as tough to handle as you might think and that the difficulties managers face with them are often a function of inexperience, a lack of will, or simply poor decision making.

If you look at many of the potential issues that managers have to deal with, you will begin to appreciate the challenges that every government manager faces on a daily basis. Let's take a look at some of them.

Budget Constraints and Difficulties

First of all, there is the government's budget cycle, which often takes one to two years from the time money is budgeted until it is eventually allocated to an individual department, agency, or administration. This built-in delay often means that by the time government managers receive their budgets, they may not be sufficient for the task at hand due to changing situations.

A good example of this was 9/11. Since no one anticipated the unprecedented terrorist attacks on our nation, the resources needed to respond to these attacks were not included in the normal budget cycle. While Congress quickly allocated hundreds of billions of dollars to ramp up the war effort and address homeland security, it did not initially budget for programs that were ancillary to these efforts, such as veterans' health care, the processing of veterans' benefits claims, and so on. The net result was that performance in these areas deteriorated; for example, VA hospitals were inundated with veterans seeking services, and the backlog of claims to be adjudicated grew to exceed a million cases.[4]

On a day-to-day basis, government managers deal with this issue all the time, and, in most cases, the reasons for the disconnect are far less dramatic. For example, it may be that the budget distribution system is flawed, resulting in some organizations receiving a disproportionately low amount of money relative to their mission. It may be that this is a lean budget year due to a national emphasis on deficit reduction or a local shortfall in tax collections, resulting in everyone suffering from cutbacks. Or it may simply be that the resources have remained stable but, due to outside forces, the workload has dramatically increased, which for all intents and purposes means that the budget is insufficient to achieve the organization's goals.

Complicated Recruiting and Management Systems

By and large, the government's employees are just as good as the private sector's. However, the systems that the government uses to hire its employees tend to be complicated and confusing, often resulting in the government taking an inordinate amount of time to bring on new employees. Moreover, because the government quite rightly gives priority in hiring to certain groups of applicants (e.g., veterans, disabled persons), selecting officials sometimes find themselves choosing candidates who are in high-priority groups but have a lower level of technical skills than other applicants.

Once the selectees become employees, they are part of a system that offers them a wide variety of rights and protections. They generally have extensive rights to grieve any dissatisfaction with their employment, either through an agency or through a negotiated grievance procedure. They can file a complaint with the Equal Employment Opportunity Commission whenever they feel they have been victims of discrimination. If they are federal employees, they can also file a complaint with the U.S. Merit Systems Protection Board if they feel that a prohibited personnel action was taken against them or lodge a charge with the U.S. Federal Labor Relations Authority if they believe that an unfair labor practice was committed. Many government employees at the state or local levels have similar rights.

To complicate matters even further, if a worker proves to be a poor employee and a disciplinary, adverse,[5] or performance action is taken against him, he has extensive rights to reply to the proposed action and then to appeal if the action is taken. These protections can make some employees feel invulnerable and can and most certainly have resulted in some employees exercising them to "grind their supervisors down," meaning that they have prevented their bosses from having both the time and energy to concentrate on managing the performance of their activities.

High-Cost Locations

Government offices are often located where their clients are. Although cost is sometimes a factor in choosing the locations (e.g., the Defense Base Closure and Realignment Commission),[6] it is not the driving factor that it is in the private sector. Although computers have certainly made it more feasible to centralize government activities to lower-cost areas, you wouldn't want to relocate a VA medical center from New York City to Muskogee, a police force from Los Angeles to Reno, or a sanitation department from Chicago to Sioux Falls. It just wouldn't make sense.

As a result, government leaders who manage activities in high-cost areas have major challenges. For example, since the salaries they offer have frequently been noncompetitive, they have generally been less able to attract top talent, and their employees have had to live farther away from work and therefore have had draining commutes. The government also tends to experience frequent turnover, cope with a statistically larger number of difficult employee and labor relations issues, and have sky-high fixed costs (e.g., rent, utilities). To make matters even worse, government officials who manage these offices invariably have a hard time recruiting key managers to work for them because the salaries offered in these locations often do not cover the cost of housing, the expense of education, and so on.

The Mindset

In my opinion, this is one of the biggest challenges facing government organizations. Far too many of its managers believe that they can't manage performance and hold their employees accountable, because it is too difficult, too time-consuming, and too painful. Moreover, those who have tried have often been frustrated by the lack of support from their superiors.

How often have you heard a senior manager say, "Better to have half an employee than no employee at all?" How frequently have you seen poorly performing activities receive large performance awards? Have you watched a rotten apple be moved all around your organization and then get stuck with him? I think you get the point. These scenarios happen all the time. They are not a result of bad government systems; they reflect a mindset that believes in taking the path of least resistance rather than dealing with performance problems.

The good news is that an organization's mindset can be changed. It is not an easy thing to do, since it involves a change in culture. However, if management has the will and skill, it is definitely doable.

Unintended Effects of Legislation

Government leaders must follow the law when managing their organizations. Obviously, we are a nation that is governed by laws, and this in and of itself is not a bad thing. Laws are the foundation of our country, and the governing laws provide us with structure and direction.

However, in my experience, political forces often drive the creation of laws, and, while this is often a good thing, sometimes laws passed to address a short-term issue (e.g., a war, a disaster) can create unintended sets of problems. Moreover, once a law is passed, it is extremely difficult to change it, especially in this day and age when Congress and our nation is so polarized.

For example, employees of my old organization, the Veterans Benefits Administration (VBA), are responsible for adjudicating claims for veterans' benefits. In a given month, they make decisions on ninety thousand or more claims. The decisions involve new claims for benefits, appeals of recent decisions, and reopened claims.

Veterans' benefits are often a political "hot potato," especially when our nation is at war, which we are today. As I mentioned earlier, the backlog of pending claims for veterans' benefits has reached a million cases, and that is often blamed on the bureaucrats running VBA. While I have no doubt that VBA has had more than its fair share of mismanagement, it is also important to note that VBA operates within a series of laws that help perpetuate a continuing backlog.

To cite just one illustration, veterans have one year to appeal a claims decision. Conversely, citizens only have two months to appeal an adverse decision on Social Security benefits. By allowing veterans an extra ten months in their appeals process, Congress has allowed a small percentage of veterans to use this time to submit all sorts of redundant and contradictory information/evidence that create inordinate delays in gathering evidence and establishing overlapping situations that preclude reasonable, timely decisions. In short, the unintended consequences of this component of the law has been to enable a limited number of veterans to consume a large percentage of available claims adjudication time that could be better used serving other veterans.

The Fishbowl Effect

Government managers operate within a fishbowl wherein virtually all of the actions they take seem to be subject to review by a wide variety of forces. For example, area and/or regional offices, as well as headquarters, are always looking over their shoulders. In addition, they have the Inspector General (IG) to deal with, as well as the Office of Management and Budget, which is an arm of the White House, and the General Accounting Office (GAO). On top of this, they have to be concerned with their local congressional representatives, whom their constituents frequently turn to when they are not happy.

Of course, let's not forget about the media, who are always looking for a good story that uncovers government corruption, malfeasance, or inefficiency. In addition, special interest and/or government watchdogs are out there looking to expose government actions that they do not approve of.

Even the people who work for these government managers may point the finger at them when they think they are out of line. For example, the unions[7] that represent government employees always keep a close eye on management to make sure that it is treating the employees fairly and is not doing anything that would harm the bargaining unit. Moreover, sometimes the employees themselves will criticize their supervisors by complaining to upper management, the IG, their local representative, or the media.

As you can imagine, trying to manage a government organization while having so many eyes constantly watching you is not an easy thing to do.

Other Complicating Issues

The aforementioned are just a few of the constraints that government managers have to deal with. Other potential challenges may include:

► *Technology.* This may involve the computer systems not being up-to-date or not talking to each other, not having the requisite security, not being flexible enough to keep up with the demands of the mission, or simply not having the right equipment.

► *Work processes.* The organization may have work processes that are inefficient or unclear or that feature too many handoffs. It may not have sufficient documentation of the processes, leading to confusion and frequent mistakes.

► *Organizational design.* The organizational structure may not be appropriate for the present situation. It may have too many layers of management or many redundancies or may simply require consolidation.

► *Physical plant.* The organization may be housed in outdated or dysfunctional space that hinders its ability to accomplish its mission, or it may have good space that is not being used as well as it should be.

► *Metrics.* The metrics may be poorly described, or they may not properly reflect what the organization is trying to accomplish. On the other hand, the organization may have good metrics but poorly written performance standards, resulting in a weak line of sight from the national level down to the local employee.

► *Information.* Data may not flow properly throughout the organization or may not be available to the appropriate people who need them. Even worse, the organization may not be able to capture essential data or may be unable to gather data on a timely basis.

► *Training.* The organization may have a weak training program that does not provide its employees and managers with the skills they need in order to thrive, or it may provide good individual training courses but not structure the training in a strategic fashion that would enable the organization to meet its long-term goals.

► *Pay.* Most government organizations utilize one or more pay systems that are relatively inflexible and tend to value time on the job over performance. While there have been pay-for-performance initiatives, they have generally been limited and have met with mixed reactions and results.[8]

► *Rewards and recognition.* The organization may not be rewarding the right performance/behaviors, it may be inconsistent in its approach, or it may be sending out messages that are at odds with the goals it is trying to accomplish.

► *The use of contractors.* In the push to reduce the size of government and/or because the government may lack certain skill sets, administrations have increasingly relied on contractors to help get the work done. One of the problems with this approach is that contractors are not civil servants, which at times makes it difficult for government managers to control their actions.

► *Management.* The organization may have a new, inexperienced, and/or weak management team that is not prepared for the challenges that confront them. This is due in large part to the exit of the Class of '73,[9] which is retiring or expected to retire soon in droves. The net result of this will be the outflow of many senior and midlevel officials, leaving the government with a slew of relatively unprepared replacements.

As you can see, there are many reasons why it is difficult to manage performance in the government. To compound matters, in all likelihood, the challenges will only increase over time, as the world becomes more complex, our country becomes more polarized, the budget deficit increases, employees become even more litigious, and the problems continue to increase in magnitude.

What Can Be Done to Improve Performance in Government?

There are many, many things that can be done to improve performance in government and address the issues cited. However, before I go forward and address those issues in the following chapters, I want to be clear that this book is primarily intended for government leaders, managers, and supervisors *who are operating within the current systems.* As such, it is not intended as a prescription for how to change government at a broad national, state, or local level. That involves a different set of challenges and requires a high degree of political involvement. For the most part, I leave that to other people who have greater expertise in that area than I have.

For that same reason, this book does not, for the most part, address legislative changes that in many cases would certainly make government work better. That is a whole other animal and is best left for someone who has more legislative expertise than I have.

Also, it does not go into much detail as to how to make large-scale improvements in areas such as technology, since that is usually beyond the reach of your typical management official and is not within my own area of expertise. Again, this is a book that is designed to help managers improve performance within their own work environment and sphere of influence.

That having been said, I strongly believe that if all government managers were to apply the principles contained in this book, that in and of itself would fundamentally improve the overall performance of government at every level. That is because there is so much room for improvement in government, due to bureaucratic inefficiencies, misaligned systems, weak accountability, poor management, and similar factors.

The point of the discussion in this chapter is that the fundamentals of performance improvement at any level are the same. They involve aligning and refining the organization's key management systems (technical, structural, decision making and information, people, rewards, and renewal—more on that later) so that the employees (1) receive a clear and consistent message as to the direction they should be going; (2) are placed in the best possible position to provide excellent service to the public; and (3) are held accountable for their actions. It also requires that a strong leadership/management team be in place to successfully implement these systems, manage its employees within this framework, and make the appropriate adjustments along the way.

Every manager who is looking to improve the performance of her unit or section should be familiar with the approach described in this chapter, learn more about the key management systems, and understand how each of the systems works in conjunction with the others. In this way, she will begin to recognize when the systems are working well and when they are not and will know how to implement the requisite fixes.

One of the key premises of this book is that high-performing government organizations work within excellent management systems, and *it is the systems that drive the right employee behavior.* That is, people will perform and behave the way that the organization wants because they receive clear and consistent messages from all of the organization's management systems. Top-notch supervisors, of course, will still need to skillfully manage their employees;[10] but *they will do best if they manage them within the framework of an integrated set of management systems.*

This book addresses all of the key management systems, with a chapter devoted to each system[11] and its implication for performance improvement. It also discusses how they relate to one another, examines different ways you can set up and modify them, and provides strategies for successfully using them. It further shows you some innovative ways to manage your employees within these systems and addresses the constraints and challenges described earlier. It concludes with a series of real-world government case studies that show how performance can truly be improved if one follows the concepts contained herein.

CHAPTER 2

Organizational Systems

I first became exposed to the concept of organization-tion systems design in the 1990s, when my office was seeking to undergo a fundamental change in its performance, culture, and approach. A new leader had arrived in our office, and he questioned the way we did business. He felt that, although we were doing pretty well, we could do a lot better, and, quite frankly, he wanted to modernize our approach to work.

Prior to that, I (and most of my peers) tended to both look at and manage performance in a very reactive manner; if there was a problem, I looked to see who was at fault and whom I should blame. As many other managers did, I tended to fault people for our performance problems and did not think to look more deeply at our management systems and how they interacted with each other.

At that time, I was unfamiliar with the thinking of the pio-

neers in the field of systems design such as W. Edwards Deming
and P. R. Scholtes.

> Deming believed that most problems in an organization
> can be attributed to a system, not to people. "In my experi-
> ence, most troubles and most possibilities for improve-
> ment add up to proportions something like this: 94%
> belong to the system (the responsibility of management);
> 6% are attributable to special causes" (Deming, W. E. "The
> New Economics for Industry, Government, Education"
> [2nd edition]. Cambridge, MA: MIT Press, 1994, p. 33).
> Scholtes add[ed] his viewpoint on the importance of be-
> coming knowledgeable about organizational systems and
> identifie(d) what is wrong with our present systems.
> Among a long list of current systems issues, which he
> call[ed] "brainshakers," he include(d) the following:
> We look to heroic efforts of outstanding individuals for
> our successful work. Instead we must create systems that
> routinely allow excellent work to result from the ordinary
> efforts of people. . . . Changing the system will change what
> people do. Changing what people do will not change the
> system. . . . The greatest conceit of managers is that they
> can motivate people . . . attempts [they make] will only
> make things worse . . . Behind incentive programs lies man-
> agement's patronizing and cynical set of assumptions
> about workers . . . Managers imply that their workers are
> withholding a certain amount of effort, waiting for it to be
> bribed out of them.' (Scholtes, P. R. "The Leaders Hand-
> book: A Guide to Inspiring Your People and Managing the
> Daily Workflow," New York: McGraw-Hill, 1998, p. ix–x.)"[1]

We brought in a consultant named Bill Snyder, who worked
at the time for Paul Gustavson,[2] the founder of Organization
Planning and Design, Inc. He immediately challenged the way
that I (and others) viewed our work and prodded us to think
differently.

He taught us to first develop a deeper understanding of our organization's underlying structure, which included its strategies, systems, and processes, and to see how it influenced our employees, our culture, and, ultimately, our performance. He showed us that this was where we needed to look to truly improve our organization. In other words, people set up the systems and such, and therefore it was up to us to change them. We had the opportunity to change many of the goals, the values, the rules, the procedures, the processes, and the structure; and if we made the right choices, we could literally remake our organization.

For me, it was one of the defining moments of my career, because it forced me to question some of my long-held beliefs and made me recognize that there was another, better, more logical and sophisticated way of looking at work and the relationship of our employees' behavior/performance to a series of key drivers. I began to see that managing people and ultimately delivering top-notch performance was more complicated than simply securing enough resources and then holding people accountable. At the same time, I also started to understand that designing, aligning, and implementing an integrated set of management systems could enable our organization to move forward in a much more focused and consistent manner than I previously thought was possible.

Virtually all government and nongovernment organizations use a series of management processes and systems to manage their operations. When these elements are properly designed to support the accomplishment of the organization's mission, vision, and values, the organization is well positioned for success on every level. In short, the processes will promote and encourage success rather than inhibit it from happening.

The process of designing and aligning an organization's systems is commonly referred to as organizational systems design. The basic idea behind it is that you get what you design for and that, if you want to change your organization's results, you need to first change the design of its systems. Phrased differently, "if you always do what you have always done, then you will always get what you always got."

This book is not about organizational systems design per se. However, as both a manager and a leader, I have found that using an organizational design model was very helpful in guiding my thinking about my organization's present and future design and, more important, its performance. As you will see in future chapters, I will be using this concept as the framework for examining and suggesting potential areas for improvement, in terms of design, implementation, and management of the workforce.

Organizational design will help you more clearly understand what is currently happening in your organization and will give you a good sense of the design choices that have been made to date and their impact on our performance. It also enables you to identify the choices that need to be made in order to create the type of organization required to achieve your future goals. It allows you to identify any gaps that may exist between where you are and where you want to be and to determine how to get there (through design and execution). Finally, it prompts you to look more holistically at the way your organization is being managed and forces you to question and ultimately rethink some of the ways that you are treating your employees.

The OSD Model

To help us frame our thinking even further, Bill also introduced us to the Organizational Systems Design (OSD) model, which was developed by Paul Gustavson. This model illustrates how organizations work in an open environment and the manner in which they convert inputs (claims filed, complaints made, applications filed for a license, etc.) and convert them into outputs (benefits granted, complaints adjudicated, licenses issued, etc.). Most importantly, it makes it clear that the organization's design choices ultimately drive its outcomes.

While there are other models in the marketplace that address similar themes, I have found this one to be perfect for my needs in terms of both assessing government organizations that I have led and assisting other organizations in my capacity as a consultant. To me, it is both clear and logical, and it literally forces you to view your organization's work in a way that you would not normally do.

Here is the OSD model:

Figure 2-1. The OSD Model

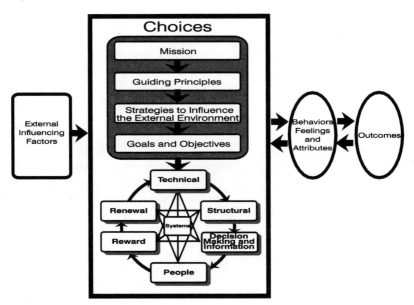

This model shows how the key elements of an organization work together to drive an organization's outcomes. The left-hand box indicates that the external environment has a major influence on the organization and greatly affects the design choices that it makes. The middle oval reflects these key choices (its mission, core values, strategies, goals, and systems), which will ultimately drive the right side of the chart: the knowledge and culture and, ultimately, the outcomes. The model makes it clear that an organization's performance flows from the choices that the organization makes. We are going to examine many of the choices, as well as strategies and techniques for implementing them, in the next chapters.

The beauty of the OSD model is that it helps one think about and understand the relationships that affect an organization's performance. This is very useful to a government manager, who spends so much time reacting to events and dealing with a never-ending set of priorities that she never really has the time to look at the big picture. The OSD model, if used correctly, will help her look more deeply and systematically at the local management systems and processes, understand their impact on the organization's culture and performance, and find new ways to improve her outcomes. Eventually, she will find that when the systems begin to work together, in lockstep, she will spend less time cracking the whip and/or putting out fires and more time actually managing her operation. She will, believe it or not, have time to actually look down the road for future improvement opportunities.

You Can Influence Design

Government managers may feel they have at best a limited impact on designing systems, and certainly that is true for national design choices. Our manager probably can't change the national mission, goals, processes, and so forth. After all, if every local manager were to do that, there would be chaos, and the organization would not be able to move forward in a clear and cohesive manner. Still, *local managers have far more discretion than they might think in terms of how their systems are designed, aligned, and implemented.*

For example, they can:

- ▶ Set local goals and determine how this information will be shared.
- ▶ Decide what to measure (over and above any national requirements).
- ▶ Look at their local work processes and make them as efficient as possible.
- ▶ Design their physical plant and make it as effective, efficient, and attractive as possible.
- ▶ Hire new employees and decide whom to promote, reassign, and detail.
- ▶ Set up and manage their local training programs.
- ▶ Establish employee performance standards.
- ▶ Administer their performance appraisal system, including firing poor performers if necessary.
- ▶ Develop and implement their local rewards and recognition program.
- ▶ Manage leave.
- ▶ Play a major role in determining the organization's culture.
- ▶ Determine how to renew their unit or section.

You are not a victim, and there are many things you can do to improve employee performance; beyond hoping that someone in Washington, D.C., or your own state or local headquarters will change one or more of the governmentwide systems or give you more resources or help to pass legislation that will make your life easier. If that happens, great; I just wouldn't count on it. Better to concern yourself with your own sphere of control, understand what you can do to improve performance, and then go for it. That is a much more liberating way of managing in the government, because you will find that (1) you will have no illusions or false hope, and (2) you have the ability to make things better.

That is not to say that there still won't be problems, because there certainly will be. You will still have to cope with many, if not all, of the challenges (and possibly more), that I listed in Chapter 1. However, you will now have a more logical approach to trying to prevent and/or deal with these problems, and in a way that is less overwhelming and more sustainable.

The point here is that you do not have to simply be a pawn in the bigger game of government. You can be a player and make a difference. The key is to have the best possible operation, because (1) that is what we all want to have; (2) the better your operation's performance, the more people will leave you alone and let you do your thing; and (3) if you are good enough, they will even come to you and want to learn from you, and what manager doesn't want to see that happen?

A Detailed Explanation of the OSD Components

Let's look at all three sections of the OSD model in more detail to see what they are and how they relate to each other.

External Influencing Factors

The external environment constantly drives changes in government organizations. Customers, unexpected events, the media, the White House, Congress, the Inspector General, other tax-payers, stakeholders, unions, and other factors can all create demands that force governments to respond and react. If they do not, events can quickly spin out of control, and the organization will wind up with a bunker mentality, hunkering down and taking blows from every angle.

How often have we seen one story take on a life of its own? The media pick up on it; oversight hearings are held; headquarters sends in a help team; and, before you know it, the entire management team is replaced. Understanding the environment will help keep you out of trouble and enable you to plan for the future.

Part of understanding the environment is learning from it. That means finding out who is the best in class (whether inside or outside government) and benchmarking with him. It might also entail learning who is on the cutting edge, implementing a new program, process, or technology, and stealing shamelessly from her if it makes sense.

The point here is that all government managers truly work inside a fishbowl. You do not work in a safe, secure, and undisturbed environment that is immune from outside forces. On the contrary, whether you realize it or not, you are constantly being influenced by and reacting to a wide variety of external forces. The more you understand this and learn how to successfully deal with these forces, the better you will be able to manage your own destination.

Outcomes

I'm now going to focus on the right side of the model, because, since an organization's performance to a large extent is a function of its design choices (as well as the skill of its leaders and management staff), it first needs to decide the overall results it desires before the design choices are made. This is the bottom line and what this book is all about, since my goal in writing it is to help government managers improve the performance of their organizations.

Before we move forward here, we need to be clear on some definitions. The OSD model uses the broad term "outcomes" to define four different types of results: customer, stakeholder, community, and individual, all of which can be measured by a series of one or more indicators. However, the GPRA makes a distinction between outcomes and outputs as follows:

Outcome Measure GPRA Definition: An assessment of the results of a program compared to its intended purpose.

Characteristics: Outcome measurement cannot be done until the results expected from a program or activity have been first defined. As such, an outcome is a statement of basic expectations, often grounded in a statute, directive, or other document. (In GPRA, the required strategic plan would be a primary means of defining or identifying expected outcomes.)

Outcome measurement also cannot be done until a program (of fixed duration) is completed, or until a program (which is continuing indefinitely) has reached a point of maturity or steady state operations.

Although the preferred measure, outcomes are often not susceptible to annual measurement. (For example, an outcome goal setting a target of by 2005, collecting 94 percent of all income taxes annually owed cannot be measured, as an outcome, until that year.)

Output Measure GPRA Definition: A tabulation, calculation, or recording of activity or effort that can be expressed in a quantitative or qualitative manner.

Characteristics: The GPRA definition of output measure is very broad, covering all performance measures except input, outcome, or impact measures. Thus it covers output, per se, as well as other measures.

> Strictly defined, output is the goods and services produced by a program or organization and provided to the public or to other programs or organizations.

> Other measures include process measures (e.g., paper flow, consultation), attribute measures (e.g., timeliness, accuracy, customer satisfaction), and measures of efficiency or effectiveness.

> Output may be measured either as the total quantity of a good or service produced, or may be limited to those goods or services with certain attributes (e.g., number of timely and accurate benefit payments).

Some output measures are developed and used independent of any outcome measure.

All outputs can be measured annually or more frequently. The number of output measures will generally exceed the number of outcome measures.[3]

For the purposes of this discussion, we will focus primarily on outputs, not outcomes, as that is what government managers, particularly those in the field, are required to achieve. These are the annual goals and targets that they struggle to meet and what this book is designed to help them achieve. The outcome goals generally fall within the responsibility of program managers at the headquarters level, and they are not usually measured on an annual basis. While the principles described in this book will also help program managers achieve their outcome goals, they are not the intended audience for this book. So, to repeat, even though the OSD model uses the term "outcomes" to describe an organization's desired performance, *in this book, we*

are referring primarily to a government organization's achieve-
ment of its output goals.

Most government organizations use either a performance
dashboard or a balanced scorecard to both establish and track
their desired performance.[4] Many of the measures are usually
established at the headquarters level, but the local manager
often has the discretion to supplement these measures if she so
desires.

These are a few examples of how these measures may be
shown:

▶ Achieves a total score of 85 or higher on the balanced
scorecard

▶ Meets at least 85 percent of the goals established

▶ Meets nine of twelve objectives, with one of the nine
being the 90 percent customer satisfaction standard

The point here is that while government managers usually
have some but not total say in the development of the performance measures, they need to be intimately aware of what these
measures are and where they come from. After all, the local
strategy and design choices that they make, along with the way
that they manage their organization, will ultimately determine
how successful they are at meeting their objectives.

A Manager's Influence over Knowledge and Culture

Every government organization needs to determine the knowledge that it needs to succeed, including new ways of doing business; finding opportunities to capture this knowledge; and then
sharing it with the appropriate members of its workforce. This

may be accomplished by first identifying the competencies required for each key position, identifying the gaps between the ideal state and the current state of the workforce, and then putting a plan in place to bridge those gaps. The next step would be to implement the plan through a variety of techniques, including classroom training, online training, webinars, mentors.

Culture refers to the behaviors, feelings, and shared values of the organization's workforce. It reflects the way people think (i.e., almost a shared philosophy), the way they approach work and each other, their norms of behavior, and so on. When organizations have aligned systems, plans, processes, and goals, their employees receive a consistent message and tend to work together with a shared purpose. In a sense, all of the organization's energy is focused like a laser beam on achieving its mission and goals. This often results in many of the employees feeling that they are part of something special, something that is bigger than all of them.

In my experience, excellent government organizations have cultures that drive their performance. Their employees are "turned on," and they want to be the best. Failure is not an option; people do not tolerate poor performance or bad attitudes; innovation is encouraged; and managers do not look over people's shoulders and criticize them every time they make a mistake. In short, the culture is a self-fulfilling prophecy of the success that surely follows.

On the other hand, organizations with poor performance are also an outgrowth of their culture. These organizations have turned off and cynical employees whose primary motivation is to make it to the weekend and ultimately to retirement. This type of organization makes excuses for poor performance, blaming it on local circumstances or the high cost of living or decisions that were made that were beyond their control. One of the reasons why the culture is so poor is that the employees see that management tolerates poor performance and bad attitudes, so they wonder why they should work so hard. Compliance seems to be an important part of this type of culture, with managers constantly berating employees to do what they tell them. Just like an organization with an excellent culture, organizations with a poor culture ultimately become a self-fulfilling prophecy.

This particular component of the model is extremely important because the outcomes (outputs) are driven by the workforce's knowledge and culture. In other words, a well-trained workforce that constantly strives for new and improved ways to achieve its mission, is excited about its mission, and has a performance-driven culture will inevitably deliver superior performance.

Strategy

This section of the OSD model refers to the mission, core values, strategies for influencing the external environment, and the goals and objectives of the organization.

Mission. In government, unlike the private sector, the mission is set by the appropriate legislative body. A government organization cannot change its mission or decide to sell an unproductive business line (although, under certain circumstances, it could decide to contract out some of its work).

Government organizations do have the opportunity to clarify their mission when they write their mission statements. By and large, they usually try to articulate their missions in clear and concise terms and in a way that expresses its overall importance to the public. For example, the U.S. Social Security Administration's mission is to "Deliver Social Security services that meet the changing needs of the public."[5]

The Los Angeles Police Department has a longer statement: "It is the mission of the Los Angeles Police Department to safeguard the lives and property of the people we serve, to reduce the incidence and fear of crime, and to enhance public safety while working with the diverse communities to improve their quality of life. Our mandate is to do so with honor and integrity, while at all times conducting ourselves with the highest ethical standards to maintain public confidence."[6]

Here is the statement of the Detroit Public Schools: "The Mission of Detroit Public Schools is to develop a customer and data-driven, student-centered learning environment in which students are motivated to become productive citizens and life-long learners, equipped with skills to meet the needs of their next customer, higher education, in the world of work."

Your job as a manager is to help the organization meet its mission. If it will help bring clarity to your local organization, you can even develop your mission statement, as long as it is consistent with the national statement.

Values. The core values reflect the organization's simple beliefs, or rules about what it represents and how it goes about its business. In other words, they express what the organization is all about. All employees should be aware of the organization's values, and managers should try to manage and behave in such a manner as to ensure that the employees are on the same page.

For example, at the U.S. Environmental Protection Agency (EPA), Administrator Jackson recently sent a clear message that the agency is back on the job. The administrator's first 100 days were shaped by three core values, which are designed to inform and guide EPA's work in the months and years ahead: "First, science must be the backbone for EPA programs. Second, EPA always must adhere to the rule of law. Finally, as President Obama has emphasized, EPA's actions must be transparent. Public trust demands that the public's business be conducted openly."[7]

As you can see, these values are more than just written words. They are intended to drive the way that EPA goes about its business.

I encourage local managers to develop their own core values, which will help shape their own organization. I certainly did that when I was the leader of a large government office. However, if you choose to create your own core values, make sure that you also incorporate your headquarter's values as well, since you are still part of the larger team and need to go in the same direction.

Strategies. The strategies to influence the environment involve attempting to meet the needs of the external environment and developing relationships with the key players in order to facilitate achieving the organization's goals. That is why government leaders must learn how to both understand and influence the environment. They need to control the "sound bite" whenever possible so that they do not get caught up in a chain of events that lead to disaster.

In my experience, every government manager needs to do at least three things to address this issue: (1) they should stay abreast of the key events that are happening in the area that they manage (both internal and external to their organization) so that they can anticipate potential problems before they happen; (2) they should develop good relations and perhaps even partnerships with their stakeholders, suppliers, and regulators; and (3) they should deliver the best performance possible, since having good performance is the best way to stay out of trouble.

Where possible, government managers should even try to shape the perceptions of the people who have an interest in their organization. After all, it's one thing to deliver good performance but quite another thing for the outside world to believe it.

For example, as the director of VA's Regional Office in Los Angeles, I redesigned that office using a concept I call visual management.[8] Working with many dedicated employees, we transformed the physical plant from a stodgy, dark, and dreary environment into one that was a loving tribute to veterans. We did this by adding history displays, memorabilia, a helicopter, a U-2 cockpit, a Willys jeep, models of a tank and submarine, a bunker, a field hospital, and patriotic music. This initiative changed our culture and reconnected our employees to the mission. However, it also shaped the outside world's view of our office so that every time a stakeholder, such as the media, visited our office, that stakeholder always viewed us in the best possible light and tended to treat us better than would have been the case had our environment remained unchanged.

Goals. The goals and objectives are discrete measures that are used to determine whether the organization is achieving its desired outcomes/outputs. These are relatively narrow performance indicators, compared to the outcomes section, which is more about overall program performance. The goals and objectives that the organization decides on are crucial to its overall success. If it selects numbers that are too easy to attain, it can be accused of setting its sights too low. On the other hand, if the numbers are almost impossible to achieve (which they often feel like they are), then the organization will demoralize its employees and set itself up for failure.

Listed here are sample goals and objectives:

▶ Actions will be processed in an average of thirty days or less.

▶ 93 percent of actions taken will be accurate.

▶ 90 percent of decisions appealed will be sustained.

▶ Customer satisfaction rate will be 85 percent or higher.

▶ Has no more than one on-the-job injury per 250 employees per year.

▶ 95 percent of patients will be seen by a medical professional within fifteen days of appointment.

▶ Arrest rate will increase by 10 percent.

The strategic decisions that government organizations make often become self-fulfilling prophecies. While local managers cannot make all of these determinations, they certainly have enough opportunities to make decisions that will position them for either success or failure. After all, for the most part, they determine their local culture, they can and should influence their environment, and they normally can choose at least some goals and objectives.

Design Choices: Where the Manager Really Makes a Difference

These are the six key management systems that every government (and private sector) organization has:

1. "The technical system deals with the organization's business processes—the activities it routinely carries out to create and deliver value for customers. It also encompasses physical arrangements for interacting and exchanging knowledge as well as technology.

2. The structural system is the way the organization is organized.

3. The decision-making and information system deals with decision-making processes throughout the organization. What specific responsibilities are given to which roles? What are the planning processes? What are the critical decisions, and how are they made? It also includes choices about the capture, distribution, and display of information.

4. The people system deals with how people are attracted, selected, oriented, trained, certified, performance managed, and promoted. It also includes career development choices.

5. The reward system is the pay and benefits structure, but also includes incentives, celebrations, and informal rewards and recognitions.

6. Organizations must be constantly learning to stay competitive. The renewal system is the way they encourage and formalize such continuous learning. What structures or processes are in place for gathering together to learn, for sharing best practices? When a problem-solving discussion takes place in an individual or team review, how do employees put the ideas generated into practice? How do they report back on the results?"[9]

It's one thing to have good systems and another thing to have them aligned. By this I mean having all of the systems working together so that the employees receive a consistent message, and work in the same direction, toward the same goals. Without alignment, you will tend to have a diffusion of energy because employees will receive mixed messages and therefore will work in different directions instead of in one fixed direction.

For example, if you want a team-based organization, it's not enough to simply put a team together and announce that you value teamwork. You need to have the right structure and the proper physical plant (e.g., you don't want everyone behind high partitions). You also need to train people on how to work together as a team. Finally, your performance standards need to credit teamwork and not simply value individual output, and your awards system needs to reward individual and group achievement.

From a manager's perspective, it is at the design choice level where the rubber meets the road. Once managers are clear about the left- and right-side components of the model, it is the middle part, particularly the design choices they make and the way they implement them, that offers the biggest opportunities for improvement; and this is where I will now focus.

The next section is devoted to showing you how to improve performance in your organization. The approach I recommend is a holistic one; instead of simply concentrating on one area (e.g., individual employee performance) the way that most managers seem to do, you will begin to look at how all of your systems are designed and fit together, as well as the way you both implement them and manage within them. The idea here is that if all of the systems work together and you treat everyone fairly and consistently within the confines of those systems, you will have a more developed and motivated workforce, which will provide you with the performance you are seeking. By the same token, you will feel less pressure and will actually have more time to breathe because the systems will be doing much of the work that you have traditionally done by yourself.

Each of the next five chapters addresses one of six key management systems identified in the OSD model (technical, structural, decision making and information, and so on). I will walk you through each system in depth, describe areas to look at, and suggest ways to improve your systems. I will also prompt you to look at how each system relates to the others in order to ensure that you have alignment throughout. Finally, I will also discuss how to implement your systems, talk about how to manage within them, and supplement each discussion with real-world examples from government.

My intent is to show how you can build and maintain a powerful set of management systems that will work together and lead to excellent performance. It is not an easy thing to do; on the other hand, it is not as difficult as you might think.

PART 2

Improving Performance

CHAPTER 3

Streamline Your Business Processes: The Technical System

As I noted in Chapter 2, "The technical system deals with the organization's business processes—the activities it routinely carries out to create and deliver value for customers. It also encompasses physical arrangements for interacting and exchanging knowledge as well as technology."[1]

Business processes are the steps and actions that organizations take to accomplish their work. Whether they are documented or not, designed or not, understood or not, nothing gets done until someone (or "the system") does it—that is what business processes are all about. They are a combination of business operating procedures, business rules, business data, and supporting technology. Yet, many business processes are undocumented, misunderstood, not optimized, not followed, error-prone, and inefficient.[2]

Improving an organization's business processes is commonly referred to as business process reengineering (BPR). The following is one definition of BPR: "Thorough rethinking of all business processes, job definitions, management systems, organizational structure, work flow, and underlying assumptions and beliefs. BPR's main objective is to break away from old ways of working, and effect radical (not incremental) redesign of processes to achieve dramatic improvements in critical areas (such as cost, quality, service, and response time) through the in-depth use of information technology. Also called business process redesign."[3]

To a large extent, in government, BPR hit its peak in the Clinton administration with its reinventing government initiative,[4] led by Vice President Al Gore. David Osborne, coauthor of the best seller *Reinventing Government*,[5] served as a key adviser to the vice president.

The mission was to review both individual agencies and governmentwide systems (procurement, budget, personnel, etc.) in order to develop recommendations for reengineering the federal government. In addition, the vice president asked agency heads to create "reinvention laboratories"—i.e., entities within each agency that would both pilot potential innovations in service and where needed and receive waivers from internal agency rules.

The goal of this program was to create a government that worked better and cost less. Its approach was to put customers first, empower employees, cut the red tape that existed at the time, and get back to basics.

The Phase I report of this initiative, "Creating a Government That Works Better and Costs Less,"[6] included 384 recommendations. It contained 1,250 actions designed to save $108 billion, reduce the number of "overhead" positions (e.g., management, procurement, human resources), and improve the overall operations of government.

Ultimately, President Clinton directed that many of the recommendations in the report be implemented, such as cutting the workforce by 252,000 positions, reducing internal regulations by half, and requiring agencies to set customer service standards. Interestingly, while the study phase of the reinventing government initiative was under way, the Government Performance and Results Act, or GPRA, which was discussed in Chapter 1 of this book, was adopted.

Around the time that the reinventing government initiative was beginning to evolve, my old office, VA's New York Regional Office, decided to take a good, hard look at its business processes. A VA regional office is the part of the U.S. Department of Veterans Affairs that adjudicates claims for veterans' benefits.

After a regional office receives a claim for benefits, it is required to gather all of the requisite evidence (which often comes from a variety of sources in scattered locations) and then adjudicate each issue claimed (e.g., post-traumatic stress disorder, traumatic brain injury, a back and/or knee problem, diabetes, hepatitis, tinnitus). It is a highly complex, paper-intensive process that involves many steps and multiple handoffs and can take months, if not years, to complete.

We brought in a consultant, Bill Snyder (the consultant I talked about in Chapter 1, who worked with Paul Gustavson), to help us conduct a thorough review of our business processes. Our director at the time had been reading about business process reengineering, and he believed that our processes were inefficient and could be greatly improved.

At the time, every regional office had many layers of management, and employees were generally organized in silos, meaning they were grouped according to their job responsibilities. In essence, the jobs were relatively narrow in scope (different people involved in the claims process were responsible for placing a claim under control, gathering the evidence, rating the claim, determining the award, writing to the veteran, authorizing the claim, deciding an appeal, and so on), most employees had little if any interaction with veterans (a relatively small customer contact team responded to inquiries from veterans), and an incoming claim moved along a virtual assembly line, although in reality it often bounced back and forth between the many hands that were involved in processing the claim. Because of the way the office was set up and the manner in which the work flowed, no one owned the claim, so there was relatively little job satisfaction and, most important, a high degree of frustration among veterans.

To make matters even worse, we were operating in New York City, which is one of the most expensive areas in the country; we were therefore in one of the marketplaces where the federal government is the least competitive in terms of salary and ability to recruit and retain top-notch employees. Moreover, that office, for the most part, had a long history of disgruntled employees providing poor service to its customers. This was the context for our decision to reengineer the way that we did business.

Working with Bill, we followed the OSD model approach to redesigning our organization. After scanning the environment; seeking the views of veterans, employees, and stakeholders; determining the results we wanted to achieve; and clarifying our mission, strategies, goals, and objectives, we rigorously analyzed our business processes and technical systems, as well as our other management systems, and radically changed the way we operated.

We decided to merge the claims processing and customer contact activities and to combine the jobs of customer contact counselor and claims examiner into one position, known as a case manager. Each case manager became responsible for handling most aspects of a claim, from start to finish, for the veterans within their individual jurisdiction. This approach gave veterans the same human being to talk to and enabled them to speak with the employee who was intimately involved in decisions affecting their claims.

This process simplified the way that a claim flowed, reduced the number of steps and handoffs, and ensured that there was greater accountability for the work performed. It also gave the employees better control of their work, more responsibility, and a greater sense of ownership.[7]

While this radical change also had its downsides (e.g., employees had to have more technical knowledge than ever in order to do their new jobs correctly, and some former claims examiners did not like answering the phones and/or being pulled away from a case to answer a phone call), our reengineering efforts proved successful enough that Vice President Gore personally gave our office the first "Hammer Award" for reinventing government.

Conducting a Thorough Review and Redesign of Your Technical Systems

I am now going to provide you with more detail as to the methodology used to make the changes I have described. Note that this approach makes the most sense for a relatively large-scale organizational reengineering project, given the potential cost (if you use an outside contractor), as well as the time and energy that is required to undergo such a comprehensive organizational analysis.

There are other approaches you can take and tools you can use to conduct a similar analysis of your work processes. However, by and large, they all come from the same general perspective; you need to take a disciplined approach and look at your processes from a distance and decide how you can best design them so that you can improve the way you conduct business.

I will also address how first- and second-line supervisors, as well as other managers, can also review their technical systems, albeit in a faster, less time-consuming, and less expensive manner, in order to quickly identify improvement opportunities in their particular work units. The point here is that there are multiple ways "to skin the cat" and improve your technical systems. The key is to select the approach that makes the most sense for your individual situation and then find ways to streamline and improve your processes.

A Simplified Approach to Business Process Reengineering

The following approach is a highly simplified version of the rigorous process that we actually went through. After all, this is not a book about organizational systems design, and I will be covering many other areas beyond that in my quest to help you improve both your organization and your employees' performance. That having been said, it is important that you become familiar with and understand the concepts so that you will at least understand the principles behind the approach I describe. I found that having a basic knowledge of systems design made an enormous difference in the second part of my career, because it allowed me to start to see how things fit together and to understand the importance of alignment. It literally helped me to think more clearly, find the root causes of problems, and find ways to resolve them.

Once again, I want to mention that the following section is heavily influenced by the work of my good friend, Paul Gustavson.[8]

Start by identifying, prioritizing, and mapping your business processes. Identify and prioritize the processes so that you know which ones are the most important and require the most resources. This will enable you to determine their impact, identify waste, redundancies, and bottlenecks in each process and to look for ways to refine it so that you can deliver your products and services in a quicker, more accurate, and more efficient manner and improve the satisfaction levels of your customers, stakeholders, and employees.

Let's look at the methodology in a bit more detail, recognizing that this is still only a brief overview of the entire process. It's important to understand that everything described herein is not necessarily done sequentially and that certain activities should be given higher priority, depending upon your situation. The key is to involve the right players, gather all of the essential information, process it, and then make the right decisions in an integrated and timely fashion.

Environmental Scan

Begin by trying to get a sense of what your stakeholders and customers feel about your organization. Try to find out what is going well and what you need to improve upon. For us, this entailed talking to veterans' service organizations, our headquarters, other regional offices, our local medical center, and other groups that were affected by our work. You should also try to benchmark your processes with best-in-class organizations that are outside your area in order to gain a broader perspective on your work.

Spend a considerable amount of time speaking to your customers. You will be amazed by how much you will learn by simply taking the time to speak with and listen to the people you serve.

Process Mapping and Analysis

Conduct a technical analysis of your business processes and map them. Use a simple grid to help you identify the gaps between each process's desired outcome and actual performance. Then look in more detail at each process that has a significant gap and potential for improvement. The idea here is to look at how the work flows and identify the points where value is created.

Value Analysis and Work Categorization

Once you have your processes mapped, you can figure out which tasks add value to the process of converting an input to the desired output. Then you can reduce or even eliminate the ones without value.

The next step is to then categorize the work. Work categorization looks at the way work impacts on the organization from a strategic perspective, providing important insight into decisions about what work should be done, where it should be located, and what resources it should receive (some areas that are typically looked at in this review, besides the direct labor, include Human Resources Management [HRM] Finance, and information technology). The work is normally categorized on a work decision tree to determine whether it is competitive, essential, nonessential, etc.

Many government agencies have chosen to centralize HRM. In my view, this strategic decision certainly saved Full-Time Equivalent Employees (FTE); however, it also devalued HRM as a career field and caused many HRM specialists to either retire or leave the field. As a result, today many managers in the government struggle to find a good HRM specialist who can provide them with sound advice.

Constraint and Variance Analyses

Another available tool is the constraint analysis, which helps identify point(s) in the process most responsible for slowing it down and/or limiting higher performance. This analysis is designed to help you identify the constraints and come up with new approaches.

The variance analysis looks at defects or deviations in the process and their impact down the road. This approach can be enormously informative because it forces you to closely examine the impact of the defects on your ability to serve your customers.

Figure 3-1 shows an example of a variance analysis chart:

Figure 3-1. Variance Analysis Chart

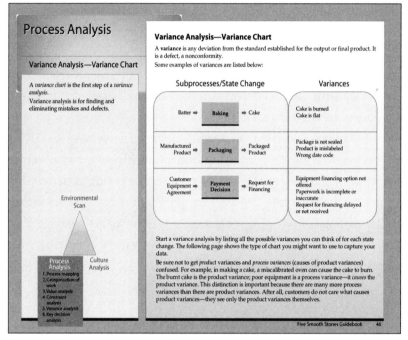

The above chart is provided courtesy of Paul Gustavson.

Process Ownership and Key Decisions

From here you can identify who will own each business process. After all, since these processes are what drive your organization's performance, you need someone to both own and manage your processes. The person selected should be able to keep the big picture in mind and understand how it works from beginning to end.

The process owners should monitor the processes, determine what needs to be done to ensure that they are operating as intended, and decide the degree of their personal involvement (e.g., in our case the person who was responsible for the appeals process looked at what we could do to reduce the number of appeals filed, how we could speed up the time it took to decide an appeal, reduce the number of appeals pending, and so on).

You should also identify the key decisions that must be made regarding your processes and assign responsibility for those decisions to the appropriate groups and individuals. The objective here is to identify the knowledge required for the individual processes and to make sure that it is properly diffused. Clarifying roles and resolving ambiguities with respect to these activities helps ensure that everyone is clear about his or her responsibilities.

This completes the technical analysis of your organization.

Cultural Analysis

The last major analysis to be conducted is a cultural analysis, which deals with how well knowledge is generated and used throughout the organization. Knowledge is developed, shared, and implemented by people through social activities and networks, and the degree to which these activities function is crucial to its ability to manage knowledge.

In this area, you conduct an individual needs assessment, which identifies the degree to which your organization is meeting the individual needs of each employee. The thinking here is that the more you meet employees' needs, the more they will be able to contribute positive energy to the organization. Figure 3-2 is an example of an individual needs assessment:

Figure 3-2. Individual Needs Assessment

Step One: Write down your answer to the following question:
I am most energized in my work when:

_____

_____

Now think of any role in life that you enjoy or have enjoyed in the past. Some examples of roles include coach, parent, choir member, fisherman, and bowling team member. Record your answer to the following question:
I am most energized in this role in life when:

_____

_____

Step Two: Share your answers with your team. Look for individual needs that your team has in common, and then list them. You could use the template given on the following page.

Step Three: Rank the needs your team has listed using a multi-voting technique. You may use any technique that you choose. One way might be to give everyone five votes. Each person distributes his or her votes in any way desired—for example, five votes to the need he or she feels is most important, or three to one need and two to another, or one vote to each of five needs. Then when everyone is finished voting, total the votes for each need. The need with the most votes is ranked first, the need with the second most is ranked second, and so on.

Step Four: As a group, determine your overall level of satisfaction (H = High, M = Medium, or L = Low) for each need.

Step Five: Discuss design choices that lowered the level of satisfaction ratings, and suggest design choices that might improve the ratings in the future.

The above is courtesy of Paul Gustavson.

You may also look at the degree to which your employees have the requisite behaviors, feelings, and attributes to deliver the outcomes you desire. In a sense, you want to determine how well your culture is aligned with your organization's mission and vision.

Finally, you should develop a skills matrix, or competency grid, which compares the skills that are needed by your employees/teams to the skills that are desired by the organization. An example of such a grid is provided in Figure 6-1.

Joint Optimization

This is where the "rubber meets the road." Here is where you take the results of all of your analyses and redesign your organization using the OSD model as the framework for your thinking. In a way, you are trying to envision how you would design the organization from scratch, which is a very exciting and liberating way of thinking.

Let me give you a sense of some of the changes that were ultimately made in our office:

- ▶ As stated earlier, we combined several jobs into one position, case manager.

- ▶ Multiple file clerk positions were combined into one position, case technician.

- ▶ We converted from an assembly-line process to one in which a single team owned the entire claim and a veteran had one point of contact. When veterans called about the status of their claims, they were able to speak to someone who was actually involved in the decision-making process, instead of someone who could give them only general information.

➤ We converted from a hierarchical organization to a much flatter, team-based one.

➤ Instead of the traditional method of resolving every issue in writing, wherever possible, we tried to resolve issues over the phone.

➤ When appropriate, we also tried to fax evidence/material back and forth, rather than always relying on written communication sent through the mail.

➤ We measured our performance using a balanced scorecard (one of the first in government), instead of a more traditional performance dashboard. For the first time, we actually measured the cost of how much it took to process a claim instead of merely noting "productivity" (i.e., the number of FTE that it took to process one thousand claims).

➤ We made some changes to the pay system, abolishing within-grade increases and using the money that was saved to reward people who could demonstrate that they had increased their skill sets.

Once you finalize your design choices, you put both a transition plan and an action plan in place to make sure that you will successfully move from your current state to your future ideal state. You need to do this because (1) large-scale change efforts always require a high degree of planning; and (2) one of your primary concerns during this time of change should be to provide good service to your customers while you are devoting an enormous amount of resources to transition (e.g., planning, training, changes to the physical plant).

Improving Your Processes Without Going Through a Major Redesign Effort

Obviously, most government organizations do not have the time, energy, staffing, money, and/or inclination to go through the type of large-scale redesign initiative that I just described. It is simply not realistic, especially for smaller activities that encompass relatively few employees and have limited control over their budgets. That having been said, there is no reason why any organization, no matter how small, can't find ways to improve its processes.

A good way to start is to become highly familiar with the concepts I just described and perhaps even to read a book or two to learn even more about the topic. Some good ones to consider are W. E. Deming, *The New Economics for Industry, Government, Education* (MIT Press, 1994); R. M. Burton, G. DeSanctis, and B. Obel, *Organizational Design: A Step-by-Step Approach* (Cambridge University Press, 2006); David Osborne and Ted Gaebler, *Reinventing Government: How the Entrepreneurial Spirit Is Transforming the Public Sector* (Addison Wesley, 1992); and Michael Hammer and James Champy, *Reengineering the Corporation: A Manifesto for Business Revolution* (Harper Books, 1994).

Improving your knowledge of this area will help you think holistically and prompt you to look at the cause and effects of your processes. As stated earlier, it will also provide you with a framework within which you can look at your systems, even if you will be examining them in a less formal manner than if you were conducting a full analysis.

Next, you should look at your metrics and see where the gaps are between your goals and objectives and your actual performance. From there, develop some quick flow charts of the processes that you suspect are in question and see if you can spot any obvious flaws.

For example, I was working with a human resources management service that had been receiving a lot of complaints regarding how long it took to fill vacancies (a more detailed description of my work with this service can be found in Chapter 8). We looked at the way that work flowed and concluded that there were several steps we could eliminate under certain circumstances. Let's look at the process in more detail:

Step 1: The activity that had a vacancy would submit a request to fill that position (via a Standard Form [SF] 52) to its Position Management Committee (PMC).[9]

Step 2: The PMC would approve, deny, or defer filling the position. It usually took the committee one to three weeks to make a decision on each request.

Step 3: The SF-52 would then go to Position Classification, where it usually took between three and thirty days for the job to be classified.

Step 4: The SF-52 then went to Staffing, which announced the job, rated and ranked the applicants, and then submitted a certificate of eligibles to the deciding official. This part of the process ran relatively smoothly.

As we analyzed the work flow, we realized that Steps 2 and 3 were potential roadblocks. Although both the PMC and Classification played an important role in the process, we recognized that they didn't need to be involved in every single vacancy. Accordingly, we identified certain positions (primarily jobs that had many incumbents and high turnover and that were almost always approved) and exempted them from going through Steps 2 and 3. The trade-off was that each service was still responsible for managing its budget, staying within its FTE ceiling, and keeping both the PMC and Classification aware of the actions it was taking. The net result of this adjustment in the work flow was that the organization filled these jobs much more quickly than it had in the past.

You should also make sure to talk to your employees and get their perspective on the work processes and flow. I believe that if you want to know how to solve the problems in your processes, the people who best know the answer are the ones who actually do the work. They are there on the front line, day in and day out; they use the processes, watch how the work flows, and see the results. Whom better to ask than them?

Let me give you a good example of how talking to the employees resulted in a major change in a process and, ultimately, in the results. An organization I was consulting with had significant backlogs in processing its work. When I asked the employees about it, they all said that the backlog occurred because every action had to go through the section's supervisor, who was already swamped with all sorts of work. I talked to her and got her to agree to allow most of the noncomplicated work (which was the bulk of the backlog) to be released once it was approved by one of her employees

The trade-off was that, at the end of each month, she would review a random sample of each employee's work in order to ensure that the quality was acceptable. The net result of this one simple change was that the organization's timelines immediately improved.

Another example involved the delivery of mail. We noticed that our mail was taking several days to arrive in our units. After looking into the matter, we concluded that the problem was not the post office but our own internal mail flow. Virtually all of our mail was being sent to one general address, so that was how it was delivered to our mailroom—in one gigantic pile. This required the workers to first sort the mail by each division, then make a second sort by section and a third by unit. Given the fact that we were receiving thousands upon thousands of pieces of mail per day, this became a burdensome and wasteful process. In essence, we were doing a tremendous amount of non-value-added work. The net result of these multiple sorts was that we were often losing a day or two or even more before the mail was being delivered to our divisions, and this was adversely affecting our processing timeliness.

The solution was to establish individual mailbox addresses at the post office for each of our divisions similar to the following: Division A—Mailbox 1; Division B—Mailbox 2; Division C—Mailbox 3; and so on. Where appropriate, we even established individual boxes by team—Mailbox 1A, 1B, 1C. We then notified our customers and stakeholders of this new approach so that they knew how to properly address their mail to us.

While there was some cost to this approach (the cost of the mailboxes), we more than made up for it by reducing the number of hours we devoted to sorting the mail and by the time we saved in delivering the mail to its proper location.

The point here is that you can improve your processes in many different ways. Sometimes the best way is to conduct a large-scale review of all your processes, especially if you are looking to review and redesign virtually your entire organization. However, most of the time you don't need to do that. As long as you stay open-minded and do not become too set in your ways, you should be able to find plenty of opportunities to improve your processes.

Ensuring That Employees Have the Knowledge and Tools They Need to Do Their Job

Another issue to look at is the degree to which the employees understand your processes. One of the things I learned in my career is that many organizations tend to spend more time developing their processes than they do communicating and explaining them to the people who do the work: the employees. As a result, far too often, good systems get undermined simply because the employees do not know how to use them. This is especially true in this day and age, when the systems are often highly complicated (due to changing laws, frequent litigation, complex technology, and other factors) and take a great deal of expertise to administer.

A few years back, this point was driven home to me by a recently appointed division chief. He took over a division that had really been struggling. In fact, it was failing to meet all of its key performance standards. After analyzing what was going on in his new division, he concluded that one of its biggest problems was the lack of understanding of and compliance with work processes. Accordingly, he began writing a series of division memoranda explaining all of the key processes and policies, distributed them to every employee, and then conducted training sessions on each; the goal was (1) to ensure that everyone understood what to do; and (2) that everyone could properly apply the processes and policies in his or her day-to-day job.

These memoranda helped bring order to what used to be chaos. For the first time that I could remember, almost everyone knew what the processes were and how to use them. People no longer could do whatever they desired; they had to do what the organization *needed them to do, and in the way that the organization wanted them to do it.* The employees now had crucial information that they didn't have before, and this contributed to a significant turnaround in performance. Within about two years, the division met all of its standards.

Writing policy statements is an excellent way to communicate information to your employees, but it is not the only way. After all, your employees have different learning styles (e.g., some prefer to learn through the written word; others prefer logic and reasoning).[10]

Another way to communicate information about your processes is to make them more visual and less wordy. After all, in my experience, not everyone is willing to weed through a 50- or 100-page manual to find a key piece of information.

One way to do this is by using flow charts. A flow chart is a visual portrayal of the steps or stages, order, and relationships involved in the performance of a function or a process. They are relatively simple to follow and usually illustrate the key decision points involved. Figure 3-3 is one of many flow charts that the IRS has developed.

As you can see, flow charts are highly visual tools for communicating information to your employees, stakeholders, and customers and will definitely reduce variances in your processes if used wisely. They can be hung up on bulletin boards, placed in a centralized binder, and/or distributed to employees.

On a different note, imagine if you developed a series of one-page learning posters for your employees, customers, and

Figure 3-3. Sample IRS Flow Chart

Figure B. **Can You Deduct Expenses for a Non-Military Move Within the United States?**[1]

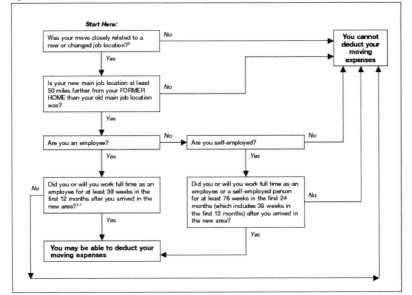

[1] Military persons should see *Members of the Armed Forces* later, for special rules that apply to them.

[2] Your move must be closely related to the start of work at your new job location. See *Move Related to Start of Work,* earlier.

[3] If you deduct expenses and do not meet this test later, you must either file an amended tax return or report your moving expense deduction as other income. See *Time test not yet met,* later.

[4] If you became self-employed during the first 12 months, answer YES if your time as a full-time employee added to your time as a self-employed person equals or will equal at least 78 weeks in the first 24 months (including 39 weeks in the first 12 months) after you arrived in the new area.

1. Military persons should see *Members of the Armed Forces* later, for special rules that apply to them.

2. Your move must be closely related to the start of work at your new job location. See *Move Related to Start of Work,* earlier.

3. If you deduct expenses and do not meet this test later, you must either file an amended tax return or report your moving expense deduction as other income. See *Time Test Not Yet Met,* later.

4. If you became self-employed during the first 12 months, answer YES if your time as a full-time employee added to your time as a self-employed person equals or will equal at least 78 weeks in the first 24 months (including 39 weeks in the first 12 months) after you arrived in the new area.

This flow chart clearly illustrates the process and is relatively easy to follow.

http://www.irs.gov/publications/p521/15040e02.html, accessed October 19, 2009.

other interested persons. Learning posters, also referred to as learning maps, pictorially show the key components of your work processes on a single page. As with flow charts, you still need to have written manuals that explain your processes in great detail. However, if you develop these posters and either give copies to your employees and/or hang them up in the workplace, you will reach more people, and people will be more likely to refer back to these posters, because they are both easy to read and easy to find.

A learning poster that I once developed can be seen in Figure 3-4.

Figure 3-4. A Sample Learning Poster

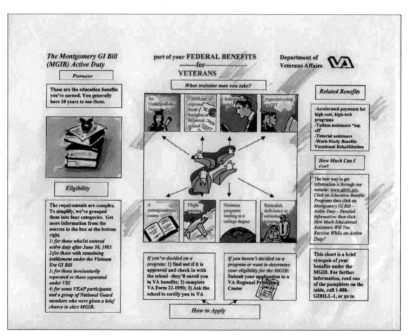

An example of a learning poster, which is more visual than a typical flow chart.

This was developed as a learning poster for veterans, not

employees, to help them understand their rights under the previous GI Bill. I developed this because many veterans had complained that they had a hard time understanding their rights under the Bill and found it extremely difficult to wade through the lengthy and complicated documents that VA had issued on the subject.

In my view, any government organization can develop similar posters for its own employees, giving them the most important information they need to know. The posters can be hung in an area near where the employees work, in much the same manner that an art store hangs its posters so that its customers can easily flip through them (they usually segregate them according to subject—movie stars, sports stars, landscapes, animals, and so on). Doing this ensures that there is a stronger base of core knowledge and demonstrates a real commitment to learning.

Naturally, you also need to ensure that there is a reasonable degree of oral communication with respect to your technical training. You can accomplish this through group training classes, conference calls, or one-on-one mentoring sessions. Talking to people in different settings ensures that there is two-way communication, which is an essential part of learning.

Other more recently developed ways of communicating technical (and other) information include online training courses (typically over an Intranet), and Web conferences, which are used to conduct live training over the Internet. During these sessions, each attendee remains at his computer and participates with others on the Net. When this happens, the students use either a downloaded application on their computers or a Web-based application that they access through a link. Depending upon the technology being used, there can often be a fairly high degree of two-way communication between the participants.

Physical Arrangements
Layout

In my view, the overwhelming majority of government organizations give relatively short shrift to their physical plant. Most offices are nondescript and are totally forgettable. In fact, when you walk into many of these offices, it is hard to tell who their customers are or why they are even there.

The desks seem to be arranged without rhyme or reason; the walls, at best, feature a bunch of photographs or reproductions of paintings that almost seem to be there as an afterthought. Moreover, relatively few if any performance data are displayed, and you rarely see any areas honoring the organization's employees. In short, very few government organizations use their physical plants to actively drive improved performance.

You might start out here by first making sure that the work is flowing properly. Once it reaches that point, you can ensure that the workspace is optimally arranged. To accomplish this, take a fresh look at how people are situated and try to rearrange them, if necessary, so that the right people are sitting in the right locations with the right furniture. While that might sound like a big task to pull off, let me give you an example of how I handled that exact situation.

One of the divisions that I was overseeing had all of the employees bunched together on the southern side of the building, with all of the file cabinets situated together on the northern side (see Figure 3-5).

Figure 3-5.

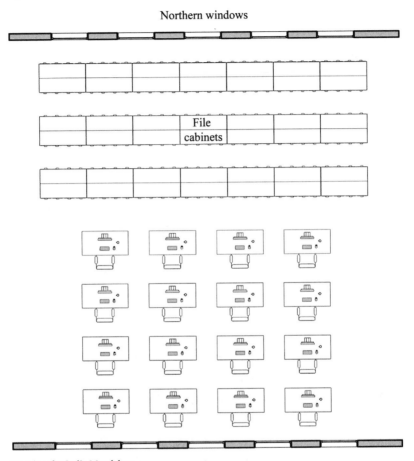

Northern windows

Drawings by Jodie Mendelson

As you can see, the employees were all squeezed together in individual desks, while the file cabinets had a great view of Los Angeles through our northern windows. Moreover, many of the employees had a hard time concentrating on their work (it was the area in our division where the most complex and highly technical decisions were made), since the way the desks were configured often resulted in other people coming into the work area to socialize. Finally, there were no partitions or other barriers to provide some degree of privacy and/or to segregate this work area from any other. The net result of this design was low productivity, as it did not adequately support our overall work flow scheme.

In rethinking the design, we felt that our employees, not the file cabinets, should be near the windows. Second, we decided to use the file cabinets as natural barriers to segregate each section and to reduce the number of unnecessary visitors coming into the work area. Third, we wanted to give the employees work stations, instead of desks, which were more modern and professional, provided the employees with more space for storage of manuals, materials, and other effects, and were more in line with our overall scheme. Finally, we felt that some of the employees needed more privacy than others, so we intentionally gave them work stations with higher partitions.

At this point, you are probably saying to yourself, "He obviously had a lot of money to buy new work stations, and I don't; so our situations are not analogous." However, that is not true; we simply went out and found organizations (both government and nongovernment) that had excess furniture that was still in good shape and picked it up free of charge. Our only cost was the expense of hauling the furniture back to our office and installing it, which was relatively low.

Figure 3-6 shows the revised design.

The first month after we made this change, we saw an 8 percent increase in our productivity.

I have talked about how high partitions for some employees were an important design choice that helped us improve our

Figure 3-6.

Northern windows

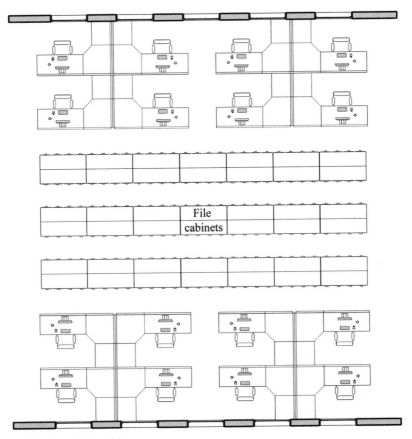

Drawings by Jodie Mendelson

performance. Let me now describe the circumstances in which high partitions hurt a government operation.

I was detailed to a large office that was struggling at the time. The organization aspired to have a team environment, but communication was poor and people were frustrated. As soon as I walked around the office, I immediately saw that one of the problems was that most of the employees were behind high partitions. Under this design, when you were sitting at your desk, the only other person that you could see was the person directly across from you. Beyond that, you could not see anyone else.

In my view, there was no business reason for having so many high partitions; all they did was hamper communication, inhibit teamwork, and make it more difficult for the supervisors to keep track of their subordinates. I strongly suspect that if the people who chose the high partitions had the chance to revisit that decision, they most likely would have decided to go with lower ones.

Lights, Flooring, and Color Scheme

Once the layout is set, you can then begin to turn your attention to what I refer to as the foundation—the lights, the flooring, and, most important, the color scheme. These elements need to work together to enable your office to have a bright, clean, organized, professional, and, ultimately, a dynamic look.

The lights might seem to be a "no-brainer," since everyone needs an appropriate degree of lighting in order to function well. However, on several occasions, usually in response to some crisis or challenge (e.g., an energy crisis, budget deficits) governments have been known to intentionally turn some of the lights in their buildings off.

When this happens, you should consider (1) redesigning some of your arrangements in order to allow more light to enter from the windows; (2) switching to more energy-efficient bulbs; and/or (3) placing an electric eye near your lights so that they go on only when there is some movement. However, these crises/challenges eventually end, and, when they do, you want to make sure that you have lighting that best fits your operation.

In 1994, I took over an organization that was housed in space that was very dark and dreary. The lighting was poor because the U.S. General Services Administration (GSA), which was responsible for managing the building, had, in 1978, turned off half the lights in response to the Iran oil embargo. When I took over that office, everyone was so used to the dim lighting that no one thought to turn the remainder of the lights back on. Upon my arrival as director, I immediately demanded that all lights be turned on, and GSA complied. People were amazed at the difference, greatly appreciated the improved lighting, and frequently remarked, "Stew turned the lights on."

Flooring is another area that receives scant attention from management, yet can make quite a difference. People walk on floors all the time, and floors are one of the first things that everyone notices upon entering a building. Given the sheer size of the floors in any building, this should be an important design element, because if the flooring is dirty, in a state of disrepair, and/or out of key with the furniture and color scheme, it will tend to suck the life out of the space.

In my view, the ideal space should have a mix of carpets and some sort of tile or linoleum. Carpets tend to have a warmer and classier feel to them, but they should not be placed in high-traffic areas because they quickly become dirty and wear out and can easily become an eyesore. I believe that they work best in office areas where employees spend most of the time sitting at their desks.

Tile or linoleum works best in hallways, waiting areas, and

other areas where people move back and forth frequently. They tend to be sturdier, are usually brighter and easier to clean, and provide a cool contrast to the carpets.

Some factors to consider in making your choices include cost, the frequency with which you may need to access the floor below your covering (e.g., to replace wiring), and the weather in your area.

I once was involved with an office that had carpet squares that were so old and decrepit that they were literally held together by masking tape. Besides being a safety hazard, they fostered the perception that we were a third-class organization that did not care about its employees. We researched our lease and learned that we were overdue for new flooring, so we advised the building manager that we wanted to replace the old squares with a mix of new carpets and bright tiles. Once he made these changes, our space looked and felt much better, and the employees began to see that we were serious about providing them with a quality environment.

The color scheme unifies your space and helps to set the tone in your office. It can play a positive role by livening up your space and making it feel both cheerful and professional; it can play a neutral role by neither helping nor hindering your physical plant; or it can play a negative role by darkening and depressing your office.

In my view, government organizations have historically done an excellent job of creating unappealing environments that have simply fostered the impression that "this is the government." From battleship gray file cabinets to off-white walls that look like they are covered in nicotine, government space to me has historically been unimaginative and at times downright ugly.

While that is starting to slowly change,[11] I wouldn't wait for your building manager or landlord to improve your color scheme. Enlist the aid of someone who understands color schemes (e.g., an interior decorator or an employee who has a background in the fine arts), take a step back and see if your current scheme (which includes your wall colors, your file cabinets, door frames, and all other elements) is a plus, neutral, or a negative. If you see opportunities for improvement, the odds are that you can make it happen.

For example, my most recent office had a horrendous color scheme, if you could even call it a scheme. The walls were painted yellow, chartreuse, and nicotine white. The file cabinets were battleship gray, and—you get the picture. It was a complete mess.

After looking at many options, we asked the building manager to repaint the walls with "whisper white." This color immediately brightened our environment and served as the base for our remaining color choices. From there, we decided to work primarily with deep blues (for our banners, some picture frames, and the backgrounds of some of our history displays) and burgundy (for our file cabinets, other picture frames, and signage), and these two colors, in conjunction with whisper white, made our environment come alive as never before. We then added splashes of green in the form of plants throughout the workspace, and this added another dimension.

The net effect of these changes was to create a more professional, functional, and appealing environment than most thought was possible in this particular space. It shaped the outside world's view that we were serious about delivering quality service, allowed our employees to see better, and made our folks feel that management was committed to providing them with a first-class physical plant. It also allowed us to establish a dress code,[12] which was sorely needed.

When we were finished with the foundation, we were well positioned to add many other visuals (e.g., customer displays, performance information, employee photographs, rewards, and recognition data), which we most certainly did. I will discuss those types of displays, including why and how we added them, the manner in which they fit together in the context of our overall design choices and how they helped us improve our performance, in future chapters.

The concept of improving your physical plant *while* using a series of integrated visual displays to support your design choices, shape the outside world's view of your organization, connect your employees to the mission, share information, celebrate your people, hold them accountable, and ultimately improve performance is what I call "visual management." To me, organizations that choose to implement a visual management program make a conscious design choice to take their organization to another level. For a more detailed description of visual management, including its foundations, the process of implementing it, and examples of organizations who use it, see Stewart Liff and Pamela A. Posey, D.B.A., *Seeing Is Believing: How the New Art of Visual Management Can Boost Performance throughout Your Organization* (New York: AMACOM, 2004).

Technology

As stated earlier, most government organizations have large, complex computer systems that share information and connect all of their field offices. As a manager, you are not supposed to tinker with these systems, since, if you make changes that are incompatible with the national systems, you may create all sorts of unanticipated problems that could harm one or more of these systems and get you in a lot of trouble.

That having been said, you should certainly note any problems with your national computer systems and bring them to the attention of your headquarters. Management needs to know the field's perspective and, in my experience, is usually interested in learning how to improve these precious systems.

At your level, there are several things you need to do to ensure that your national systems run smoothly. First of all, make sure that all of the employees receive adequate training on the systems. This seems simple enough, but recognize that if employees don't understand how to properly use the system, all sorts of problems will start to show up (e.g., you will lose productivity because the employees will have to slow down, and quality will diminish).

Second, make sure that the employees update the system as intended. After all, a computer system is only as good as the information that is put into it. For example, our national organization implemented a computer system that was intended to enable any office in the country to answer our customers' questions regarding its individual claims. The intent was to provide us with maximum flexibility so that we could move phone inquiries at any one time to the offices that had the largest capacity to handle these calls.

Very quickly, we learned that the computer system did not contain enough information to allow our employees to answer many of the simplest questions. In short, our organization had a national compliance problem because employees across the country either did not understand what was required of them or did not think it was a high enough priority to fully populate our computer systems with the requisite information. The solution in this case was to (1) reemphasize the importance of inputting data; (2) reinforce this message with additional training where required; (3) advise the employees that we were going to track their compliance by conducting random reviews of their inputting; and (4) take disciplinary action against anyone who did not comply.

When trying to implement a national computer system at the local level, try not to take too heavy-handed an approach (although we were required to do just that in the last situation). The better approach is to do the necessary homework, prepare the workforce for the change, and then properly implement and maintain the system. In my view, most national computer system implementations develop problems because they don't take these precautions. That is why, when such a change is implemented, it is always a good idea to assign responsibility for such a change to one individual. Let this person do the planning, coordinate the training, oversee the implementation, and ensure that things go smoothly. Also, you will need to have a "go-to" person during the early stages of the implementation so that the employees know whom they speak to for answers to their questions. Depending upon the scale of the project, this may be the same person who is responsible for the entire project, or it may involve one or more experts who will be there to assist her.

While you don't want to tinker locally with the national systems, you still want to develop local programs that can assist you with your performance. These may involve simple spreadsheets, which will help you perform complex mathematical calculations or simply track the performance of your employees, or they may involve databases, which can help you track information.

For example, we often used locally developed spreadsheets to track our budget, ensure we were not overspending, and decide when we could bring on a class of new employees. We also used spreadsheets to track both individual and group performance (at both the employee and the contractor levels), until a national system was devised that provided us with similar data.

We frequently used databases to measure work that was in the hopper, such as the number of jobs we were trying to fill. The database allowed us to measure how much time it was taking for us to fill vacant positions and to further measure how long each step of the process was taking. We also used databases to keep track of certain, special-interest customers (e.g., such as how long they were waiting to be contacted, how long it was taking them to receive benefits) so that we could provide them with first-class service.

Reorganize the Activities That Affect Performance: The Structural System

The structural system is the way that you are organized. Activities that are well organized maintain effective control of their work, keep variances in their processes down to a minimum, use their resources effectively and efficiently, and have a high degree of communication. They are structured in a way that promotes collaboration and teamwork when required and are designed to enable decision makers to be as close as possible to their customers and to provide them with excellent service.

While this book is designed primarily to teach government field managers how to improve performance within their individual areas of responsibility, it is important to look at both the entire organization's structure and the structure under the control of the manager, since the overall structure impacts heavily on the local organization. The better you understand the overall structure and the rationale behind it, the more you will be able to adapt locally.

For example, if you understand where the true power is in the structure, you will know whom you need to forge relationships with so that you can get things done when you need to or where to go to influence the organization's policies. Moreover, at some point in your career, you may be in your organization's headquarters making decisions about its structure, so it's better to learn how to do this now.

In my experience, organizations with the best structure use a clear set of principles to help guide the decision making. Principles ensure that the thinking is clear, consistent, and focused.

While there is plenty of information out there on this issue, I found that the Minnesota Department of Health has put together a particularly good set of guidelines that should work well for most government organizations. Here are the principles that it used to help design its structure:

- ▶ "Organizational structures should be as simple and understandable as possible.

- ▶ Organizational design decisions should be made first on the basis of department-wide perspectives and needs, then on the division or section needs and perspectives in order to optimize resources and our ability to achieve optimal efficiency.

- ▶ When new programs or functions come to the department, the first consideration should be whether they can be integrated into existing organizational and management structures and hierarchies. If programs are not located in a division (e.g., Executive Office level) an adequate level of administrative support must be provided.

▶ Organizational structures need to be fluid, responsive and adaptive to change. Some functions because of their sensitivity or stage of development may need special visibility in the organizational chart.

▶ Organizational structures should reflect the natural flow of work and assist in the elimination of handoffs and redundant activities.

▶ Structures should facilitate the identification of work processes, pinpoint accountability for decisions and facilitate efficient management decision making.

▶ Organizational structures should reflect and be consistent with how our clients and customers experience us and internal organizational walls should be as invisible as possible.

▶ Structures should facilitate decision making as close to the point of contact with our internal and external clients as possible.

▶ The formal organizational structure should support professional development and innovation.

▶ Structures should facilitate integration and coordination among related functions.

▶ The organizational structure should help to ensure communication and the availability and exchange of information across the organization.

▶ Structures should facilitate collaboration between units, staff, management and stakeholders. They should minimize the number of layers of management and each layer should add value to the organization's ability to achieve its mission.

- ► The number and sizes of organizational units is determined by the work to be done and one size does not fit all situations.

- ► To the extent possible, internal support functions (e.g., communications, facilities, finance, human resources, information technology, legal, and legislative support) that cut across the entire organization should be grouped together to ensure efficiency and effectiveness.

- ► Seek information about what organizational arrangements are working well, and act to preserve them. Do not move boxes around unless doing so would fix a problem."[1]

As you can see, these principles are very consistent with the overall approach to designing an organization as articulated by the OSD model, which I described in earlier chapters. Interestingly, it is also very similar to the approach we took when we designed VA's New York Regional Office and ultimately received Vice President Gore's Hammer Award.

The principles are clear, logical, and holistic and focus on the big picture, as well as on collaboration, communication, efficiency, effectiveness, and accountability. Moreover, they are designed to deliver customer-focused service and to put power in the hands of the people closest to the organization's customers. Organizations that use principles such as these to design their structure(s) will make decisions that are sound and logical and will contribute to enhanced performance.

An organization's structure is typically depicted in an organization chart, which shows the rank and relationships within the organization, and explains who reports to whom. Usually, organizational elements that are shown on the same line within the chart as others are perceived to have the same degree of status or rank within the organization.

It is important to recognize that organizational charts have their limitations, as they merely show the organization's formal reporting structure. What they don't show is the organization's informal power structure, which is often built upon personal relationships and can sometimes circumvent or even subvert the formal structure.

In most cases, government organizations have several levels of organizational charts; one shows the overall organization and its individual business lines, staff offices, field organizations, and so on; one shows each business line and staff office in more detail; one shows each field installation; another illustrates the sub-elements of each field installation (e.g., each division or service).

Overall Structure for an Entire Organization

Virtually all government organizations operate within some form of a pyramid, meaning that the higher you go up the pyramid, the more power you have and the greater the number of people who report to you, either directly or indirectly. These days, however, many government organizations are so complicated that it can be difficult at first glance to see the pyramid, especially since many of these organizations now have multiple functions and a wide variety of staff offices.

In my view, there are a number of factors that should be considered in designing a sound overall structure for a government organization.[2] First of all, the lines of authority should be clear (i.e., everyone should know to whom they report). This also means that the role of headquarters (aka central office) should be clear relative to the field. Normally, headquarters should be responsible for policy, strategy, program development, coordination with the appropriate legislative bodies, demand creation (ensuring that the organization's customers are aware of the products and services being offered and are using them as intended), and oversight. The field is usually responsible for policy implementation and performance delivery. Naturally, there is plenty of overlap between both institutions (headquarters, of course, also has to focus on performance; the field also interacts with legislative bodies and tries to create a demand for their products and services).

Throughout my career, I found that, by carefully studying the organizational decisions made at the national level and the ultimate impact of those decisions, I could spot evolving trends that I could apply locally. For example, if the nation was moving toward a centralized design model, it was better to apply the same model locally, since it was surely going to be required at some point. Moreover, I also learned to study the impact of national decisions on performance, since the same lessons ultimately apply at the local level.

A major concern in designing organizations is scope; organizations shouldn't want to have so many elements reporting to one individual that she becomes overwhelmed or can give only a limited amount of attention to many of the elements. One way to handle this is to have multiple elements report to an individual, such as a deputy assistant secretary, a deputy undersecretary, a deputy director, or an assistant division chief, who then reports to the top official in the organization. The downside of this approach is that you create an extra layer of management between the elements reporting to this individual and the top person.

The same thinking should apply when local design choices are made. If you are adversely affected by these choices, you need to raise these concerns with upper management.

Another consideration is the number, size, and location of both line and staff offices. For example, are the line offices (those that deliver your products and services) located where the customers are, and, if so, do they really need to be there in this day and age of advanced technology? Would it make sense to close and/or move some of the offices to lower-cost areas in order to save on overhead and rent, be able to recruit from the top of the labor pool, and reduce your turnover? What about the political ramifications of a major consolidation? What would the outcry be like? How would the union(s) react?

Does the organization need to have multiple staff activities (e.g., human resources, finance, mailroom, information technology) throughout the organization? Can it save money, ensure more consistency, and free up FTE that could be redirected to direct labor through consolidation?

Centralizing Work Teams

With respect to performance management, there is always some degree of tension around the role of headquarters in this area. For example, if an organization has multiple product lines that are delivered in a field office, that particular field office usually reports to a director, who then answers to an area or network office, which is responsible for performance management. There is nothing wrong with this approach as long as it is recognized that every design has its pluses and minuses.

The plus side is that field offices in which multiple business lines or programs are grouped together tend to focus on overall service to their clients, which is a good thing. They, in a sense, offer one-stop shopping to their customers, which can be highly desirable from the standpoint of customer satisfaction. In addition, there is generally more interprogram communication and cooperation under this approach, simply because people from different areas work near one another. The net result of this option is that each local business line tends to stay less in its silo and is more likely to work with other lines and thus offer better service.

The problem with this approach is that the headquarters' program offices, which are responsible for setting policy, are sometimes left out of the performance management process, which is managed by an area or network office. This can result in a disconnect among policy development, implementation, and performance management and have a profound impact on the employees in the field. In other words, employees sometimes feel a bit divided because they seem to be serving two different masters—their area/networks offices and the various program offices that set policy.

One also has to question whether colocating multiple business lines in the twenty-first century still makes sense in all cases. After all, technology often makes it easy to move work from one location to the other, while making things transparent to the customer. The key here is to look at the organization design from a holistic point of view and then design the entire organization in a way that is effective and efficient and allows it to meet the needs of its customers, stakeholders, employees, and taxpayers.

These same decisions also need to be made at the local level.

In many cases, you will have the opportunity to either partici-pate in the decision-making process or at least influence the decision. Often, your degree of involvement will ultimately be a function of how well you understand the principles of systems design.

A Word About Contracting Out Work

During my career, I witnessed an enormous amount of con-tracting out government work to the private sector or to an-other government entity. In fact, quite a few government organizations have viewed contractors as an important part of their extended structure. Many, if not most, of these initiatives have made perfect sense, especially when the government orga-nization did not have the requisite expertise to perform the work and/or when the private sector or other government en-tity could do the job at lower cost.

Some of the activities that I have seen contracted out have included security work, laundry services, property manage-ment, payroll, and building management. The idea here was to allow the organization to concentrate on its core mission and to farm out the support work to someone else. In most cases, this worked pretty well, although the transition was often pretty challenging.

For example, when contracting out, you need to determine what you will do with the employees whose jobs are affected. If only a few are involved, that is usually not a problem. However, if a large number of employees are impacted and they all cannot be absorbed within the organization, you will have a different set of problems on your hands. In fact, you may have to resort to a reduction-in-force (RIF) in order to address your excess employees, and, believe me, having lived through several RIFs, I can assure you that they can get very ugly.

Another issue you will have to deal with is managing the transition. After all, while contracting out work in order to save money sounds good, the process is rarely neat and clean. Once the affected employees know that the work is being contracted out, they are usually more focused on finding another job than they are on keeping the work flowing. That is not to say that they will intentionally do a bad job; they will not, because the vast majority of government employees have enough pride in their work that they will continue to try to do a good job. However, during the transition, people will take more leave than usual and try to or actually find other work; they will tend to be a bit sloppier because of the uncertainty of their situation. The point is that while the organization will be expected to continue to do good work during the transition, you shouldn't be surprised if you see some or more than just some slippage.

Furthermore, remember that contractors are not infallible, either. That is because it's one thing to write up a successful bid and quite another thing to then pull it off. On several occasions, I've seen contractors take over work that they were woefully unprepared for, resulting in a rapid deterioration of service relative to the government's performance.[3] Moreover, even when the contractor is quite good, there is usually a fairly lengthy period where the contractor has to get up to speed—learn the technical aspects of the government's program, train its own employees, develop its computer systems, and so on.

The purpose of this discussion is to alert government planners who are considering contracting out to some of the pitfalls that can occur. Whereas there is certainly a place for contracting out, it is important to recognize both the strengths and the weaknesses of such an approach in the context of an overall government structure.

Short-Term Contracting

Another approach to contracting out work is short-term contracting. Under this scenario, a function is not contracted out in its entirety. Rather, the organization contracts with someone to perform a specific task or function for a finite period of time. For example, this might involve performing a management study, setting up a computer system, or zeroing out a backlog of unprocessed mail.

The advantage of this approach is that it quickly fills a need by bringing desired expertise into the agency for a limited period. In a sense, it's like bringing temporary employees into the organization, except that the contractor is not technically a government employee. To me, there are times when this approach works better than hiring temps, because (1) the contractors are experienced at handling short-term projects; (2) they normally specialize in certain areas; (3) you can often bring the contractors in more quickly than temporary hires; and (4) they can usually get up to snuff more expeditiously because projects of this nature are what they do. The downside of this approach may be cost, because the overall price for contractors is usually higher than for temporary employees because of the overhead involved.

I like to think of this approach as providing the government with much-needed flexibility. The decision to use contractors and/or temporary employees should be driven by the needs of the organization, costs, the ease and speed of finding such help, and similar factors. While short-term contractors may not appear on your organization chart, keep them in mind as part of your informal organization.

The Local Structure

Designing a local structure is obviously not as complicated as setting up a national structure. The scope is smaller, and fewer activities and employees are affected. Moreover, the local organizational structure should be consistent with the national structure and direction, so you shouldn't have to reinvent the wheel. However, if local managers absorb the lessons described earlier in this chapter, they will be able to apply them locally and improve their structure and ultimately the performance of their organization.

With this in mind, you should still use the same basic principles in designing your local organization as you would if you were designing your national organization. You want to have a lean, effective, and efficient organization that utilizes its resources in the best possible way to accomplish its mission. You also want to have one where there is good communication from top to bottom and where the bureaucracy is kept to a minimum.

Let's look at an example of an organization chart at a typical government agency. Note that all of the six units shown in the chart have the exact same mission. The numbers shown in parenthesis represent the number of FTE employees assigned to each activity.

When you look at this chart, several things jump right out. First of all, the office of the division chief is very top-heavy. Does he really need a support staff of six FTE (two program analysts, two management analysts, and two secretaries) to help

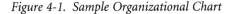

Figure 4-1. Sample Organizational Chart

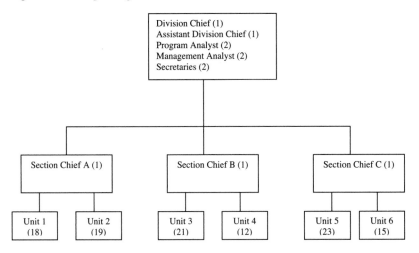

him manage 111 employees? I would assign half of these employees to direct labor activities in order to boost their capacity.

Also, why have two units reporting to one section chief? Doesn't this just add an extra layer of bureaucracy to the mix? I would abolish the section chief positions, flatten the organization, and have the unit chiefs report directly to the assistant division chief.

Note that most of the unit chiefs have a supervisory ratio of close to 1:20 or higher. This is much too high, as the ratio should generally be 1:15 or lower.[4] In fact, over the past few years, the governmentwide range has generally been well below 1:10.

That is not to say that low ratios are necessarily a good thing, as some private sector companies successfully operate with much higher ratios.[5] However, given the situation at this typical government organization (i.e., less-than-optimal computer systems, teams at stage one in their development, heavy external scrutiny), relatively low ratios made sense at that time.

I would create several more units, detail some of the former section chiefs to unit chief positions, and reduce the span of control to an acceptable level.

Let's review what the new chart would look like:

Figure 4-2. Revised Organizational Chart

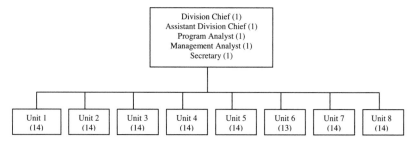

As you can see, the new organization is leaner and flatter, with one less layer of supervision. In addition, because several of the section chiefs are assigned to units, the span of control within each unit is reduced, ensuring that there is better oversight and control. Finally, with several of the support positions being rerouted to direct labor jobs, the division has more horsepower to accomplish its mission. All of these changes will result in a tighter, better aligned, and smoother-functioning division.

There are other structural areas you can look at beyond the examples I just cited that may yield additional improvements. For instance, how many clerical employees do you have relative to your professional and administrative employees? In my view, there are different ways of looking at this issue. On the one hand, clerical employees are cheaper than professional and administrative employees, so this approach can generally buy you more FTE and free up your higher-graded employees to focus on the more complex work. When this approach works well, you normally enjoy some efficiencies.

On the other hand, there are often hidden costs to having a large number of lower-graded employees. For example, they tend to have a higher turnover rate, particularly in high-cost-of-living areas. This means that you will spend a disproportionate amount of your time hiring and training them. Second, I have found that clerks often require more disciplinary or adverse actions than their higher-graded counterparts, mainly because they often come from the lower part of the labor pool.[6] Finally, if you have many clerks, you may also experience some quality challenges, since some of them may be inexperienced or have a weak command of basic business skills.

All of these factors should be considered when you are designing your organization. In my view, sometimes you may need to even design your workforce around the available labor pool. In other words, I would be more inclined to have a higher mix of clerks to professional and administrative employees if I knew that my pool of clerical applicants was strong.

Other Factors to Consider

Workflow

One other thing to consider on this issue is the workflow itself. Remember that every time you split work between a clerk and someone else, you are adding another handoff to the process, which can be problematic. Also, ask yourself if there are ways to reduce the clerical work through technology. For example, if you have an electronic records system, you won't need a bunch of clerks to establish files or find folders. That having been said, you will still need some clerical overhead to scan all of your records into the computer system, although some organizations find it advantageous to contract this work out.

Although there is no best way to handle every situation, you should at least be aware of the issues I have outlined, as they will help you make the right decision for your organization.

Grade Creep

Another subject to look at is grade creep. By this I mean that many government organizations have found that the average grade of their employees has climbed over the years. This has happened for many reasons; some of the jobs may have become more complex, there may have been a reduction in the number of clerks, government managers may have upgraded employees in order to keep them, or there may have been a lack of attention to sound classification principles.

If the average grade is increasing for the right reasons, (i.e., through planned management action in response to changing demands or technology), there is nothing wrong with that. That is the way that the system is supposed to work. However, if the average grade is creeping up unintentionally, or intentionally but for the wrong reasons (e.g., to try to subvert the classification system), the organization may have a different set of problems on its hands.

First of all, the higher your average grade, the less money you have to hire additional employees, meaning that your capacity will not be as high as it could be. Second, if your grades are going up on a piecemeal basis, meaning that some people are rewarded with higher grades in order to keep them while others are not, you may create hard feelings and a sense that the same rules don't apply to everybody. If this happens, the true cost of those promotions may be a lot higher than you think because you may wind up with other hidden costs in the form of grievances, EEO complaints, and lower morale.

I have grappled with this issue throughout my career and tried to be very careful when I upgraded one or more employees. I tried to make sure that my decisions were transparent and that everyone understood what I was doing and why. When people hear that there is a legitimate business reason for an increase in grade(s), they can accept it. They have a much harder time accepting a decision to upgrade people because of their relationship with management. When that happens, watch out.

The point here is that the way you manage your grade structure can have serious ramifications throughout your workforce, so be careful about the way you handle this critical area.

Direct Labor Employees

Another way to look at your structure is to determine the percentage of your employees that are involved in direct labor or, phrased differently, that add value to the process. In my experience, high-performing organizations tend to have relatively little overhead compared to lower-performing ones, making them leaner and more responsive and leaving them more resources to turn to.

For example, I recall studying one underperforming organization that on paper had about 70 percent of its employees devoted to performing its direct mission. The rest were supervisors, trainers, quality reviewers, analysts, secretaries, and what appeared to be nothing more than gofers. When you then factored in time that was devoted to meetings, training, special projects, leave, workers' compensation, union business, and so on, it was clear that this organization was devoting less than 50 percent of its resources to accomplishing its mission. No wonder it was experiencing performance problems!

The solution here was to redirect as many employees as possible into direct labor[7] and to eliminate all the unnecessary meetings we could; to streamline the training time so that it was both effective and efficient; to do a better job of managing and controlling leave, especially unplanned leave; and to reduce the number of employees on workers' compensation.

The point of this chapter is to show you that there are many, many ways to improve your organization's structure so that it will perform better. Although an organization chart is an excellent way to depict the organization's actual structure, you should continually examine it and the forces beneath it for improvement opportunities, especially since it has to be viewed as a living, breathing, and constantly changing document. After all, your workforce does not remain static, since people come and go; therefore, you should, both formally and informally, make subtle or even more far-reaching changes in your organization in order to ensure that it is living up to its potential.

Using Metrics to Track and Improve Performance: The Decision-Making and Information Systems

The decision-making and information systems reflect the choices that are made about the capture, distribution, and display of information. Along these lines, metrics, in particular, have become increasingly important in government, as leaders have recognized that "you get what you measure" and that "if it can't be measured, it can't be managed." With the continued push for accountability and results throughout government, metrics have taken on a more pronounced role in tracking performance.

A solid set of metrics not only measures the performance

and effectiveness of a program but also provides information that can be analyzed and used to identify problems, support requests for investments, and justify the use of additional funds that can be targeted to the areas that need improvement.

That having been said, I have been struck by what appears to be a seemingly never-ending increase in the number of metrics now being used. For example, when I first started out as a senior leader, a few key metrics (maybe a dozen or so) were used to assess the performance of my organization. The general feeling at the time was that these metrics provided a good sense as to how our organization was doing. However, by the time I left government, the number had increased to more than thirty. Some of my former counterparts are now assessed on 100 or more metrics, which, as you can imagine, makes their jobs quite difficult.

There are two schools of thought on this issue. The first one says that you measure as many activities as you can so that you will know exactly what is going on in your organization and be able to assess the overall performance of the organization, both its leaders and employees. The second one says that you measure only a few key activities, because if too many are measured, the managers will become overwhelmed and will be unable to focus.

In my view, the answer lies somewhere in between. Measuring as many activities and processes as possible is definitely a good thing, because it gives management the information it needs to identify problems upstream so that it can prevent them from becoming problems downstream. On the other hand, if you measure too many areas, it becomes tougher and tougher to concentrate on the key priorities. I recommend tracking as many processes as you can but keeping the number of items to measure as part of the performance appraisal system down to a manageable number. This provides everyone with the key information needed to manage the workload, while ensuring that people are still held accountable for achieving the organization's priorities.

What to Measure

In my experience, the best way to measure performance is through a balanced series of measures that provides an accurate view of the organization's performance and health. I advocate measuring five broad categories of performance: (1) customer satisfaction; (2) quality; (3) timeliness; (4) productivity, or unit cost; and (5) employee satisfaction and development. Let's look at each of these measures in more detail.

1. *Customer satisfaction.* This looks at the organization's performance from the customer's perspective. It is normally based on a periodic, random survey of your customers and measures the elements that are important to them. These surveys are usually conducted from one centralized point, often with the help of a contractor, and they measure the customer satisfaction of each appropriate office in the organization. Smaller, more frequent surveys can also be done at the local level to provide quicker feedback, since the centralized surveys are costly and usually are not conducted more than once a year.

2. *Quality.* This measures the accuracy of your products and/or services. It is normally determined by a review of a random sample of the work and may be done either at the local site or, more likely, from a centralized location.

3. *Timeliness.* As stated earlier, this is a measure of how long it takes the activity to perform its key actions, from the customer's perspective.

4. *Productivity/unit cost.* Productivity measures the amount of resources (usually FTE) it takes to complete an action, deliver a service, and so on. Unit cost takes the productivity measure one step further by tracking how much it actually costs per unit.

5. *Employee satisfaction/development.* This metric captures the degree to which your employees are engaged and/or motivated. This is usually done by surveying the employees on a series of different dimensions, such as their satisfaction with their jobs, their supervisors, their training, and their opportunities for improvement. Employee development measures the ideal competencies required for an organization and then compares them to the actual competencies of the workforce.

While these measures are not all-encompassing, they are similar to what you will find in most government agencies. Also, note that these are simply broad categories of measures; within them you would use more specific measures (e.g., for unit cost, the cost to answer a phone call, the cost to treat a patient, or the cost to process a tax return; for timeliness, the average time to answer a phone call, the amount of time it takes for a patient to be seen by a physician, or the average number of days it takes to receive a tax refund).

Many organizations use the "SMART" method when designing their metrics. The SMART method uses metrics that are:

- *Specific* in that they target the area you are measuring.
- *Measurable* in that you collect data that are clear and accurate.
- *Attainable* in that it is reasonable to expect an employee to achieve that metric given the available resources, tools, and so on.
- *Relevant* in that you are measuring information that is within the scope of the employee's job and that is something over which he has control.
- *Time-bound* in that it tracks the length of time taken to deliver a product or service.

SMART metrics are precise, easy to understand, realistic, and provide organizations with an excellent picture of their actual performance.

Lagging and Leading Indicators

If possible, each category should have two types of measures: lagging and leading indicators of performance. Lagging indicators tell you how the organization has already performed. In other words, they show historical performance. Conversely, leading indicators are barometers of future performance, because they give you a good sense as to how the organization will do in the future with respect to that particular area of performance.

Examples of lagging indicators include the average days to complete an action, the quality of completed actions, the productivity or cost to complete an action, and customer satisfaction. All of these measures reflect work that has already been completed.

Some leading indicators are the average days of your pending work, employee development (improved employee skills can be a predictor of future performance), and the lost call rate (this can influence your customer satisfaction score).

In my view, the most accurate sets of metrics feature both types of indicators. In this way, you get the best possible sense of the state, health, and performance of the organization. Otherwise, if you focus on only one type of indicator, you can easily get a skewed view.

For example, if the organization focuses only on the average number of days to complete an action, the employees are likely to work a disproportionately high number of newer actions. This is because the average number of days to complete newer actions will always be lower than the average number of days to complete the older, pending actions. At least over the short term, this is the easiest way to achieve that goal, unless you have already done an excellent job of controlling your work and the average age of your pending work is also low.

On the other hand, if you have metrics that include both the average days to complete an action and the average days of your pending actions, then the employees will have to concentrate on achieving both metrics. This will result in a more balanced approach and, more important, better service to your customers.

Capturing the Information

To the maximum extent possible, performance data should be captured in an electronic system. By this I mean that the IT systems should automatically gather information about all of the key indicators, in lieu of having employees manually enter this information into the system. After all, that is the fastest and most efficient way of gathering the information, and, quite frankly, the most credible way, as well. A good rule of thumb is that the more performance data are electronically captured, the more accurate they will be.

That having been said, certain data may have to be entered into your system manually. For example, the results of a centralized quality control program, wherein a quality reviewer examines completed work, have to be input manually. This will be credible as long as the reviewer is objective and has no stake in the results of the review, other than wanting it to be accurate.

The performance information should be tracked in a centralized database so that the organization will know how it is doing on each of its metrics on a national basis (or statewide or localitywide, as appropriate). It should also be able to then stratify that same information by area or region, by field office, by division or service, or by some other method. Ideally, the organization should even be able to take that information down to the unit level and, ultimately, to the employee.

The system should also contain historical performance data, dating back at least several years, preferably by month or some other normal interval that is measured. In this way, organizations can see how they are trending and compare how they are doing against how they did at similar time periods in past years. This is important because some government work can be cyclical in nature (e.g., the work may increase or decrease when school is in session or during the summer).

The information should be posted in the organization's Intranet so that all of the appropriate employees know how their office is doing relative to the goals and to others. This promotes both healthy competition and (we hope) prompts internal discussions wherein best practices are shared.

You may also want to post limited performance information on the Internet so that your customers and stakeholders know how you are doing and what to expect. Bear in mind that this approach has both plusses and minuses. On the positive side, you will be sending a message that your organization is transparent and has nothing to hide. That is generally a good thing for government to do, as open government often results in better government.

The flip side is that sharing a large amount of performance information often opens you up to greater examination and increased criticism, and no one really likes that. Advocacy groups, stakeholders, the media, and other interested parties will now be able to see your dirty laundry, and every piece of data that you display can and will be used against you. In the long term, the constant scrutiny will make your organization perform better; but, from a government manager's perspective, it can be painful.

National Versus Local Information

The systems I just described are usually designed and implemented at the national (or statewide or localitywide) level, as they should be. After all, an organization's headquarters needs to have one national performance information system that captures all of the appropriate data for each of its locations. Headquarters needs this information to measure, track, appraise, reward, improve, and budget for performance, as well as to respond to inquiries from a wide variety of interested parties.

The system needs to be consistent throughout the organization; when you are comparing "apples to apples," it is easier to spot trends across stations and to ensure that the same rules apply to everyone.

By the same token, managers at the local level sometimes need more information than is contained in the national system. It may be that they have a unique problem that is not captured in the national system, or it may be that they want to simply capture additional data points that will help them manage their day-to-day work. The point here is that if local managers feel they need more information than the national system provides them, they should go ahead and do just that.

I do want to add a couple of notes of caution before you plunge ahead on this front. First of all, as I stated earlier, make sure that you are not doing anything that would conflict with your national computer system. In other words, don't try to add locally some additional elements (e.g., software, hardware) to your national system without obtaining the requisite permission; the additions you make might conflict with the national system and cause it to stop operating properly. As you can imagine, that would be a very bad thing to do and could easily get you in trouble.

Also, be very sensitive to any privacy issues. The last thing you need to do is to violate the Privacy Act, Health Insurance Portability and Accountability Act (HIPAA),[1] or the Financial Information and Security Management Act (FISMA).[2] It is simply not worth it.

With this in mind, if you need to gather additional performance information at the local level—and I was a big advocate of that—then gather and maintain it in a local database, spreadsheet, or other file that is separate and distinct from your national system. In my situation, I not only wanted to know how many claims our organization processed each day and how quickly we were doing them, I also wanted to know how many claims were coming in to each team on a daily basis and how quickly each team was addressing them. Such an approach did not conflict with our national systems; it simply added to our knowledge base.

I used this method time and again, and it worked for me. For example, we developed a report card that tracked the performance of several of our contractors. Since these contractors were an integral part of our vocational rehabilitation process, we needed to know exactly how they were doing and what they were contributing to the rehabilitation of our clients. At the time we started doing this, their work was simply reflected in our overall performance, but it was hard to tell how they were doing and whether we were getting a good bang for our buck. By building these report cards, we were able to differentiate their contributions to the process from ours, enabling us to pinpoint any deficiencies that existed.

Remember, knowledge is power, and the more you know about your operation, the better you will be able to manage it.

Making Sense of the Information

Once you have the information you need, you should try to put it into perspective. By this I mean that you will need to decide how you can best arrange the information in order to make sense of it. In my experience, two basic ways are generally used to deal with this issue: (1) You can arrange the information on some form of a dashboard; or (2) you can arrange the information on a balanced scorecard. Let's examine each approach in more detail.

The Performance Dashboard

A dashboard is "really a performance management system. It communicates strategic objectives and enables businesspeople to measure, monitor and manage the key activities and processes needed to achieve their goals."[3]

A performance dashboard displays all of the performance indicators side by side so that the viewer can get a good sense of the overall performance of the operation. One of its strengths is its simplicity; it is relatively straightforward and simple to understand.

The dashboard provides multiple insights into the performance of an operation and enables its users to (1) track performance on each of its key indicators; (2) examine performance issues from different perspectives and provide management with the opportunity to try to fix them; and (3) provide management with a context for making decisions that will lead the organization in the proper direction.

Many government and private sector organizations use such a dashboard, as they have found it to be relatively easy to implement and simple to explain. Moreover, the most effective ones then try to link this information to their other key systems, such as performance appraisal and rewards, so that each system is pointing its employees in the same direction.

The following is an example of a government dashboard that tracks performance from many different angles:

As you can see, the dashboard clearly shows how the orga-

Figure 5-1. Performance Dashboard

Measure	Rating Related Actions (Completed)	Rating Related Actions (Pending)	Non-Rating Related Actions (Completed)	Non-Rating Related Actions (Pending)	Fiduciary Activities - Initial Appt & Fid-Ben Exams	Fiduciary Activities - Initial Appt & Fid-Ben Exams	National Accuracy Rate (core rating work)	National Accuracy Rate (authorization work)	National Accuracy Rate (fiduciary work)	Cost per Compensation Claim Completed	Cost per Pension Claim Completed	Cost per Active Compensation Case on the Rolls	Cost per Active Pension Case on the Rolls	Overall Satisfaction	Customer Orientation	Appeals Ratio	Telephone Activities - Abandoned Call Rate	Telephone Activities - Blocked Call Rate	Employee Development Matrix	Employee Survey (mean score)
Goal	186	187	45	75	715	40	90	85	90	249	96	121	161	80	90	2%	4%	4%	TBD	4%
Actual	190	174	44	91	697	50	82	81	87	569	255	183	266	75	80	13%	9%	6%	TBD	3%
Met?	N	Y	Y	N	Y	N	N	N	N	N	N	N	N	N	N	N	N	N	NA	Y

nization is doing on each of its metrics. It is easy to see whether the organization is achieving each goal, because a Y (for yes) or an N (for no) is shown right below the actual performance. These days, many dashboards add color to the cell of each metric, with green meaning the goal has been achieved, yellow denoting that the goal has not been achieved but the organization is either within 10 percent of the goal or is at least making progress, and red indicating the performance is unacceptable.

The Balanced Scorecard

"The balanced scorecard is a strategic planning and management system used to align business activities to the vision and strategy of the organization, improve internal and external communications, and monitor organizational performance against strategic goals."[4] The concept received enormous attention after the publication of the book *The Balanced Scorecard: Translating Strategy into Action*[5] and continues to do so today.

The idea here was to use a series of measures from a variety of perspectives in order to provide managers and executives with a more balanced view of an organization's performance. The perspectives that Norton and Kaplan recommend managers use are (1) the learning and growth perspective (to see how well the organization is learning and developing); (2) the business process perspective (the organization's internal processes); (3) the customer's perspective (comparing the customer's expectations to the level of service received); and (4) the financial perspective (such things as unit cost and productivity).

The balanced scorecard is intended to operate as both a management and a measurement system that helps organizations to express and drive their vision and strategy. It provides information about their internal processes and external results in order to foster improved performance and outcomes. When properly implemented, the balanced scorecard both drives and measures the overall performance of an organization.

Figure 5-2 shows an example of a government balanced scorecard.

This scorecard contains the same basic information as the dashboard, but it displays it in a radically differently way. It is a bit harder to follow than the dashboard, but, in my view, it provides you with richer insights. Let's look at the differences between the two approaches in a bit more detail.

Comparing the Performance Dashboard to the Balanced Scorecard

It is clear that the scorecard is more complicated and harder to understand than the dashboard. That is because the scorecard is a richer and deeper instrument, and it is more complicated to design and, ultimately, to understand.

Figure 5-2. Sample Balanced Scorecard

Category	SPEED						ACCURACY			UNIT COST				CUSTOMER SATISFACTION					EMPL. DEV. & SAT.	
Weight	21%						28%			16%				20%					15%	
Measure	Rating Related Actions (Completed) (2)	Rating Related Actions (Pending) (7)	Non-Rating Related Actions (Completed) (2)	Non-Rating Related Actions (Pending) (7)	Appeals Resolution - Average Days/Case (2)	Fiduciary Activities - Initial Appt & Fid-Ben Exams (2)	National Accuracy Rate (core rating work) (4)	National Accuracy Rate (authorization work) (4)	National Accuracy Rate (fiduciary work) (4)	Cost per Compensation Claim Completed (5)	Cost per Pension Claim Completed (5)	Cost per Active Compensation Case on the Rolls (5)	Cost per Active Pension Case on the Rolls (5)	Overall Satisfaction (6)	Customer Orientation (6)	Appeals Ratio (2)	Telephone Activities - Abandoned Call Rate (2)	Telephone Activities - Blocked Call Rate (2)	Employee Development Skill Matrix	One VA Survey (mean score) (6)
Strategic Objective	74.0	78.0	17.0	44.0	365.0	1.0%	96.0%	96.0%	96.0%	$249	$96	$121	$161	90.0%	90.0%	2.0%	4.0%	4.0%	TBD	4.0
FY 2001 Target	186.4	187.2	45.0	75.0	715.0	5.0%	74.0%	68.0%	65.0%	TBD	TBD	TBD	TBD	59.0%	68.0%	8.0%	7.0%	4.0%	TBD	3.7
Zero Value	200.0	150.0	125.0	100.0	1,000.0	43.0%	35.0%	35.0%	35.0%	$550	$280	$215	$300	35.0%	35.0%	13.0%	35.0%	50.0%	TBD	1.0
Actual	190.4	174.2	44.2	91.3	697.4	23.6%	65.0%	51.9%	58.6%	$569	$255	$183	$266	53.4%	62.2%	12.7%	9.0%	5.7%	TBD	3.4
Earned Points	0.4	0.0	2.2	0.3	2.9	0.9	7.9	2.2	1.6	0.0	0.0	1.4	2.8	2.0	3.0	0.1	2.5	2.9	TBD	4.0
Maximum Points	5.0	3.0	3.0	2.0	6.0	2.0	16.0	8.0	4.0	4.0	4.0	4.0	4.0	6.0	6.0	2.0	3.0	3.0	10.0	5.0

Target Score - EOFY	42.0	x1.35	56.8
Total Score	36.9	x1.11	41.0
Maximum Score	90	x1.11	100

NOTES:
(1) Reflects monthly
(2) Reflects FYTD data (thru current month)
(3) Reflects FYTD data (thru prior month)
(4) Reflects 12-month cumulative data
(5) Updated quarterly
(6) Updated annually
(7) End of month snapshot

This scorecard was actually used in FY 2001 to measure claims processing performance. It weights five different dimensions of performance and converts them to one overall score, with 100 being the highest possible total.

This scorecard measures performance relative to 1) a strategic objective (the first row on the left below the word "Measure"), which represents the desired performance several years in the future and if achieved, would provide the maximum score; 2) the FY 2001 target, where the organization wants to be at the end of the fiscal year; and 3) a "zero value," meaning the performance is at a level that is unacceptable and the organization receives no points at all on this measure. Thus, for performance under the category entitled "Customer Orientation," the organization's performance (62.2%) is roughly halfway between the strategic objective (90.0%) and the zero value (35.0%), so the organization earns ½ the maximum number of points (6.0/ 2 = 3.0).

Note that the target score-end of fiscal year (EOFY), the total score and the maximum score shown at the bottom left-hand side have been adjusted to account for the categories marked TBD, meaning the actual measure was still to be determined at the time.

The best way to describe the two approaches is by analogy. To me, the dashboard is like a report card from elementary school, whereas the scorecard is more like a report card from high school or college. In elementary school, the student receives a grade on each of her classes, but none of the grades is weighted, and there is no overall score given.

On the other hand, a high school report card assigns a weight to each class (usually called a credit), and the student's grades are then multiplied by those credits; for example, an "A" is usually worth a score of 4.0. If a student receives an "A" in a class worth three credits, then the student receives 12 points (4.0 x 3 = 12) for that class. After that, the aggregate score is divided by the total number of credits, which then produces one overall weighted score for the semester, year, or total time of enrollment. This overall score is commonly referred to as a student's GPA, or grade point average.

To me, that is one of the strongest arguments for having a balanced scorecard, at least for the type of scorecard I have just described—you are assigned one overall score that lets you know exactly how you are doing and where you stand. I have found this approach to be much better and much more revealing than a dashboard, which simply lists your performance in a wide variety of measures. After all, if there are thirty, forty, or even fifty or more measures on your scorecard, and you achieve 50 percent, 60 percent, or 75 percent of them, how do you know if you are doing well? Moreover, how do you know which ones are the most important? The scorecard both simplifies and clarifies matters by assigning weights to all of the measures and then rolling them up on all categories into one overall score. I found that this approach makes more sense, and, more important, *it ensures that the organization focuses on overall service, and not just on internal processes.*

I also found that the scorecard is an excellent driver of performance, because the weights assigned to each category clearly let the organization's managers know what the priorities are and where to concentrate their efforts. At the same time, they know that every point on the scorecard is precious, because their rating and potential rewards depend on their total score, so they are required to manage every metric.

Another advantage of the scorecard is that you can roll it up or drill it down to virtually any level of your organization. In other words, you can have a national scorecard for a program that produces one overall score. If you use the same measures and weights at every level, you can have a scorecard that produces one number for each division, each section, each unit, and even each employee. Imagine having such a clear line of sight! You can even have a scorecard that weights the scores of each program (you can weight it by FTE, dollars, or whatever makes the most sense for you) to provide you with one overall score for your entire agency.

Of course, you can also drill a dashboard down to low levels in your organization as well. The downside of this approach is that you drill down only by measure, not by overall performance.

I am a big fan of having one overall number, because this adds a great deal of clarity to both the performance appraisal and rewards and to the recognition systems. If people are aware of the number they have to shoot for and know there are reliable consequences for exceeding, meeting, or failing to meet it, they will have faith in the systems, the organization, and their superiors—and how often does that happen?

On the other hand, if that doesn't happen, your employees will spend a disproportionate amount of time talking among themselves and griping about how inconsistently management is treating everyone, and who wants that to happen? Sadly, in my experience, that is what usually happens.

I don't want you to infer from my comments that a dashboard is a bad thing, because it certainly is not. In fact, for most of my career, the organization I worked for used a dashboard, and it served its purpose relatively well. The biggest advantage of the dashboard is its simplicity, because people at virtually every level of the organization can quickly grasp it. The scorecard involves more permutations and calculations and takes a lot longer for your employees to grasp. In fact, in my experience, some people never master all of its intricacies.

That having been said, I believe that, in many cases, a balanced scorecard is a better instrument for the reasons I just described. It gives you a deeper and more well-rounded view of your organization, as it focuses on overall service delivery.

The choice, of course, is ultimately the organization's. The best way to look at it is to ask how the measurement instrument the organization chooses fits within the other design choices it makes. That is the question that should always be asked whenever a design choice is made.

Sharing Information

Once a decision is made as to what will be measured and how it will be displayed, the next step is to decide how the information will be shared. To me, this is an underused and underappreciated opportunity, and one that government managers rarely take advantage of. I am constantly amazed how often I visit organizations and see virtually no evidence of their performance. I'm sure that, to at least some extent, the information is available somewhere: in a computer system, a file cabinet, someone's desk, or somewhere. I'm also confident that most of the supervisors are at least vaguely (if not intimately) familiar with their organization's actual performance.

However, I rarely see the performance information displayed anywhere, which makes me wonder how important overall performance actually is to that organization. After all, if the information is not posted in one or more prominent locations, how do most of the employees know how they are doing? Moreover, what message does it send to the workforce if no one takes the time to share the information?

I believe that most government organizations should post essential performance information in a series of key locations. By doing this, it (1) lets both the employees and visiting customers and other stakeholders know that performance is important; (2) keeps everyone in the loop so all employees know what is going on and can see how their actions impact the organization's performance; (3) creates internal discussion and debate from within and helps to generate ideas for improving things; and (4) fosters a sense of transparency throughout the organization.

Posting information is not as simple as it sounds because there are many factors to consider, such as what data to post, how to post them, and who will post them. Let's look at each issue in more detail.

What to Post

Simply put, you should post as much information as is appropriate and helpful for the audience with whom you are intending to share the information. Most government organizations have several business lines and varying degrees of responsibilities. I learned early on that if you overwhelm your employees with too much information, especially information they do not understand and have no control over and no real interest in (e.g., the work of a different business line, an activity in which they are not involved and with which they have no relationship), they will become overwhelmed and/or turned off by the information and will ultimately tune you out.

That is why I believe in posting different degrees of information in different locations, depending upon the audience. The key is to maintain a clear line of sight with respect to the information posted; in other words, you provide the widest and most all-encompassing information to your highest level officials, and, as you go further and further down into your organization, you provide more narrow and focused information.

I typically like to start off by establishing a war room, which becomes the command or nerve center of the organization and contains all of the key metrics for each and every business line. This room is similar to the one that NASA or the Pentagon uses, although it is probably not as large or as high tech. The room is plastered with information about performance and projects and is the primary location where senior management meets, reviews information, analyzes problems, and plans its strategy.

The next level down is at the division or service chief level, from which a business line is usually run. Most of these activities normally have their own conference room, and they often have several supervisors reporting to the business line head. I recommend using the conference room as a mini–war room and posting all of the line's key metrics within it. The room should have charts and graphs that show how their internal processes are working, as well as trend analyses and other data—everything that one would need to know to effectively manage a business line.

The chief holds all of his staff meetings in the mini–war

room and has his subordinate supervisors view the posted information and try to make some sense of what is going on. As discussion ensues about the best course of action to take, it is always easier to make an informed decision when the requisite information is right there in front of you.

The third level down involves the individual team. I don't envision teams having their own war rooms, since teams usually don't have their own meeting or conference rooms. If they have one, great; if not, I see two options: (1) Use the supervisor or team leader's office, if she has one, as a mini–war room; or (2) use a bulletin board in an area where the team meets in order to discuss team performance.

This room or, more likely, bulletin board should contain all of the team's goals and metrics, as well as other important internal processing information. It should be focused and contain data about what the team members have control over and, ultimately, what they will be held accountable for. The team should hold its performance meetings in this area so it can discuss what is going well and what can be improved. In the same way that the war room is the command center for upper management, the team meeting area should be the focal point for discussions about team performance.

In summary, sharing performance information is crucial to an organization's success. The keys are these: (1) There is a clear line of sight from the highest level of the organization down to each individual employee; (2) the information is easy to understand; (3) the information is meaningful to the employees because they have some control over the outcome; and (4) the employees will be held accountable for the results, meaning that results will impact both their appraisal and rewards and recognition.

How to Post the Data

Organizations that post data usually place the information on bulletin boards, and that works just fine. Bulletin boards provide a neat, clean, and professional look, which is something you always want to strive for. Just make sure that the look and feel of your boards are consistent with the rest of your physical plant in terms of color and décor.

I strongly recommend that you avoid posting information directly on your walls. When you post charts and graphs on walls, they tend to look scattered and unprofessional, and it creates the impression that they were posted as an afterthought. Moreover, if you've hung paper on walls with some form of tape, pins, or glue, when you take them down you invariably pull paint off the walls and make them look worn and unattractive.

A different variation on the theme is to hang paper on cloth partitions. The advantage of this approach is that the papers don't leave any marks when you change the display. However, in my view, posting information on bare partitions still leaves you with a cluttered and unattractive look. Therefore, I still recommend using bulletin boards, even if you want to display information on cloth partitions.

A more modern and exciting look is to post computer and/or television monitors throughout the workplace. This provides a colorful and jazzy look to the physical plant and, more important, allows you to update the data automatically, instead of taking down and putting up paper documents on a periodic basis.

Who Should Post the Data

One of the questions I often receive concerns how much FTE is involved in putting together and posting all of this data. The answer is, not much, and certainly way less than one FTE. Developing graphs and charts and then posting them is not a lot of work, especially for someone who knows what she is doing.

Moreover, I do not recommend going down this path unless you see the value of relentlessly tracking data and then sharing it with the key players. In other words, don't do it because it is something that sounds like it is a good thing to do. Do it only if you believe it is the right thing to do for your organization.

Getting back to the question of who should do the posting, in my experience I have found that it should be the person in your organization who is responsible for maintaining and tracking data, such as a management analyst, a supervisor, or a team member. It doesn't really matter who that person is, as long as it is someone who does this regularly. My recommendation is that you have a schedule for developing and posting your charts and graphs that corresponds to your information tracking system or your performance goals. Whether it is weekly or monthly or a different time frame, the most important thing is to stick to your schedule.

Postings should be followed by meetings with the appropriate people to review the data and to decide where to go from there. If you do this, you will find that tracking, posting, and managing data will become a normal part of the way your organization works and will lead to improved performance.

The point of this chapter is that if you use information to your advantage, it will work for your advantage. If you do not, it will become harder and harder for you to control events and, ultimately, performance. I strongly recommend that you embrace your decision-making and information systems and make them a regular part of the way you do business. I'm certain that if you do this, you will be in a much better position to address problems well before they blow up into major disasters. Furthermore, by keeping your employees in the loop, you will help them feel more engaged, and you will have far more eyes than ever before looking for ways to improve performance.

CHAPTER 6

Recruitment, Selection, and Development: The People System

The people system addresses the way that people are recruited and selected, the way they are oriented and trained, and the manner in which their performance and behavior are managed.

Recruitment and Selection

Recruitment and selection are related to improving your performance. You would think that would be self-explanatory, but these connections are not immediately obvious. Of course, everyone wants the best talent. However, it's not so obvious that recruiting methods set the scene for how an employee will view the organization or that it can make the other employees want to work harder. In my experience, organizations that place a premium on recruiting top-notch people and promoting employees when they have earned it, not because they have been around for a while, send a powerful message to everyone that they are all about performance and achievement.

Recruitment and selection should be an important part of an organization's people plan and should be done strategically, not haphazardly. By this I mean that an organization should know its turnover rate, be aware of the employees who are eligible to retire, plan for people to leave, and design its recruitment plan accordingly. It should not passively wait for employees to leave and then start the recruitment process each time a position becomes vacant. That is simply too slow and inefficient an approach.

Along these lines, I strongly believe in what I call anticipatory recruitment, that is, recruiting to fill positions *before* they become vacant. I advocate this approach because it allows organizations to replenish their workforce while the employees they expect to leave *are still there,* allowing for a smoother transition and less disruption of services than if organizations fill positions after they become vacant.

How and when should an organization do this? First of all, anticipatory recruitment works best for multi-encumbered positions, because they have more employees and provide greater flexibility. After all, in most cases, unless you have an unusually good budget or excess FTE, it does not make sense to backfill a one-of-a-kind or two-of-a-kind position, unless you know for a fact that an incumbent will be leaving shortly. Otherwise, you will be spending more money than you probably have.

However, with multi-encumbered jobs, if you expect a certain number of losses per year, you can calculate the amount of money you will save through these losses (e.g., the length of time you will not have to pay for these positions because they are or will become vacant, the difference between the salaries of the departing employees and the salaries of the new ones) and then use this money to bring on one group of employees rather than one or two employees at a time throughout the year. If you take this approach, you will need fewer people to train the new employees, since they will be trained as one class, and as a group they will get up to snuff more quickly, resulting in better continuity of service.

With this in mind, as you plan your recruitment efforts, decide in advance the groups of people and the skill sets you would like to have for the positions you expect to become vacant.[1] This approach, wherein you decide what the end state should look like and then work your way back, is an excellent strategy whenever you plan.

In government, there is always a certain number of governmentwide recruitment procedures you need to follow. For example, in the federal government, most vacancies have to be announced through www.USAJOBS.gov. Many state and local agencies take a similar tack.

In addition, there are often internal procedures to follow, as well as legal requirements (e.g., veterans' preference), union contracts, and other factors that place further constraints on your flexibility. The best I can recommend in this area is to learn the applicable system as well as you can and then use it to your advantage whenever possible. In my experience, the systems provide a lot more flexibility than most managers think. The problem is that most don't even know enough to ask the right questions.

For example, I was recently speaking to a group of managers who were lamenting the fact that they couldn't find qualified veterans (the job was legally required to be filled by a veteran) for a GS-13 position. When I suggested that they try announcing the job as a GS-12/13,[2] meaning that the position could either be filled at the GS-13 or the GS-12 level with a qualified veteran,[3] they were stunned, because they hadn't thought about this approach.

The point here is that while the government's recruitment systems do have their constraints, they also have plenty of flexibilities, and you should use them if you need to. For instance, you may decide in advance that you want to target veterans as a possible recruitment source. Such an approach makes perfect sense for many reasons: Our government owes a major debt to veterans; they generally bring a strong work ethic, have plenty of experience working under pressure, and can be quickly hired under one of the government's special recruitment authorities (e.g., the Veterans' Employment Opportunities Act of 1998, a VRA appointment). You can reach this group by placing advertisements in veterans' magazines and/or on veterans' websites or by working with VA's Vocational Rehabilitation and Employment Division or your state's Department of Labor. By using one or more of the special hiring authorities for this or another group, you can speed up the normally time-consuming process because you won't have to wait for the traditional civil service certificate.

Other potential groups with special appointing authorities that you might want to consider targeting include people with disabilities and outstanding scholars. You can reach people with disabilities through the state's Department of Labor or through various organizations, magazines, and websites that serve this group. The best way to attract outstanding scholars is through college job fairs or with advertisements sent to each school's placement office.

On the other hand, there are times when you may want to target groups of people who do not have a special hiring authority but who would make unusually good fits for your organization. For example, positions that require incumbents to speak Spanish should be advertised in Spanish-speaking communities. You might also want to target the elderly and/or students for certain types of seasonal and/or part-time positions.

The point here is that your recruitment efforts should not be based on the presumption that you will be able to find the right candidates by simply advertising in USAJOBS.gov or your state or city's website. Better to decide in advance the type of people you are looking for, develop a plan, market your organization to your targeted groups, and then go out and find them. After all, if you don't know where you are going, you will never get there.

There are several other points that I want to make about the screening and selection process. First of all, once applicants apply for positions, they go through a two-step process. The initial step involves determining whether candidates meet the minimum qualifications for the job. This might seem simple and straightforward, but these decisions are crucial, because if too many people are found to be unqualified, your pool of potential selectees will quickly drop precipitously. To a large extent, all the process involves is comparing the education and experience of the candidates to the qualification standards.

However, in my experience, far too many HRM specialists take an overly strict-constructionist approach to this step and often screen out more candidates than is necessary.

As I see it, the key is to apply the standards consistently to all applicants, but the HRM Department has some discretion in how it interprets and applies the standards. It is like a baseball umpire: Some have wide strike zones, while others have narrower ones. What is important is to treat every batter and pitcher the same way.

I believe that HRM specialists who work in high-cost areas where there are relatively few applicants[4] need to take a somewhat looser interpretation of the standards than specialists in low-cost areas, where the pool is generally much larger.[5] This is especially true for lower-grade and trainee positions, where for all intents and purposes the government expects to train the new hires anyway. This is simply a smart but fair real-world approach to dealing with the challenges that government managers have to live with.

The second step involves ranking, which occurs when management has to distinguish the best-qualified candidates from the merely qualified ones. The key here is to devise a system that can efficiently and effectively spot differences among applicants. That usually involves comparing each applicant's knowledge, skills, and abilities relative to the job requirements and then determining who the highest-ranking candidates are. This is easier said than done, because whatever method you use to make these distinctions (e.g., multiple-choice questionnaires, written responses to questions, screening interviews), all have their pluses and minuses. For example, people often choose the highest possible response on the multiple-choice questions because they believe it will give them the best score. Written responses often tell you who the best writers are and not necessarily who the best-qualified people are. This is a tough one, and it is why I encourage you to work closely with your HRM advisers to ensure you use the system that works best for you.

First Impressions Count: Your Office Environment and Performance

When a prospective employee walks in the door for an interview, what kind of impression do you want her to have? Do you want her to see a typical, dark, grungy, and undistinguished-looking government office that makes her squirm and think to herself that even if she gets the job she is going to keep looking? Or do you want her to walk into the space, gaze up at walls that almost breathe the mission, honor the employees, and send a powerful message that performance is valued in this organization? I think the answer is rather obvious; the obvious point is that the way your physical space is designed can send a powerful message to prospective candidates.

I've already mentioned the importance of using visual displays, so I am not going to address this here in much detail. My only point is that your physical plant can be a turnoff to prospective candidates, or it can be a proactive tool that helps attract employees to you organization.

For example, my last organization had a training room that was also used to celebrate our employees. All around the room we hung pictures of our employees, including our teams, the managers, union officials, former employees, the children of our employees, employees when they were in the military, and so on. Not only were these photos well received by our employees, but when employees from other offices used to visit us, they would see them and compare our room to similar rooms in their offices. Needless to say, their offices did not compare favorably. On several occasions, after seeing our space, an employee actually wanted to transfer to our office. We took what most people barely see—the walls of a government building—and turned them into a recruitment tool.

Using Past-Performance Questions

When going through the interviewing process, organizations should focus their interviews on the past performance of potential employees. This is because past performance is generally the best indicator of future performance. I therefore recommend that you develop performance-based interviewing questions for the interviews you conduct (e.g., tell me about the time you had a problem with quality and what you did to fix it; describe a problem you had with one of your customers, and explain what you did to satisfy her). Such questions will give you deeper insight into the applicant's past performance and provide you with a better chance to project what his future performance might be.

Part of the interviewing process also involves candidates evaluating whether your organization is a good fit for them. After all, if you spend your time, energy, and money on hiring someone who later decides that the organization is not for him, the organization will have wasted its investment and will be back to square one. Accordingly, I recommend that whenever you interview someone for a job, you have that person spend several hours on the job with an experienced employee to see if the job is a good fit. Better to find out now that the employee will not be a good fit than later on.

Once you have completed the interviewing process, properly applied all of the appropriate civil service rules and regulations, and tentatively made your selections, don't forget to check the background of the leading candidates. You would be amazed how often shady people who are skilled at giving excellent interviews get selected because government managers fail to take the time to check their references.

Let me give you several examples of government managers who were caught off guard and selected the wrong candidates simply because they looked good. On one occasion, a longtime government employee was selected to be an EEO investigator. The problem here was that her supervisor had not checked with her previous office, which might have advised him that she had just admitted retaliating against another employee for filing an EEO complaint.

On a separate occasion, a government supervisor selected a candidate for a trainee position without looking into his background and/or looking closely at his SF-171 (the official application form used at the time to apply for jobs with the federal government). It turned out that he had been convicted of murder. While he was eventually removed from the government, a lot of time, energy, and money were wasted on his situation.

Orientation and Training

An employee's first year on the job is usually considered to be the last part of the examining process. This is because it provides the government with the opportunity to watch the employee and determine whether she is a good fit. By the same token, it also gives the employee the chance to evaluate whether she wants to stay with the government for the long term.

The first chance you get to shape a new employee's view of her organization is during orientation, where the employee gets to learn all about it and meet some of her co-workers. Take advantage of this opportunity and hold your new employee orientation in a quality location that sends the message that you are a first-class organization. By all means, do not hold it in some dumpy room, away from everything, that gives the impression that orientation is merely an afterthought; if you do that, the employee will be talking about this experience for years to come.

Make sure the employees who speak at orientation have good people skills and are excellent representatives of the organization. The last thing you want is to have some cynical bureaucrat drone on and on in a monotone to your new employees.

Make the orientation enjoyable and inspiring. For example, show a video from the national, statewide, or citywide head of your entity that provides an overview of the entire organization. Have the local leader come down and introduce himself to everyone. Make sure he shares the mission, vision, and core values with the employees.

Show a film that traces the history of your organization, and follow that up with a tour of the local environment. Have an HRM specialist come down and explain all of the benefits, programs, rules, and regulations that will affect each employee. Give them plenty of time to ask questions and to fill out the appropriate paperwork.

You might even want to pair each new employee up with a more experienced coworker. In this way, she will have someone who will show her the ropes and a buddy she can turn to for questions.

The point here is if you make the effort to start the employee off on the right foot, the odds are that she will in fact do so. That is one reason why organizations such as the Walt Disney Company do so well. They invest in their employees, starting from the moment they begin work there, and inculcate their values in each person. If you take the same approach, you will be way ahead of the game.

Training and Development

Employee development should be an integral part of your people plan, not a haphazard, off-the-cuff adjunct to which you occasionally send your subordinates. Unfortunately, that is how it often seemed to happen during my career.

Looking back, I think that occurred because many of my supervisors thought of training as something they had to do because it was mandated from above. In other words, they grudgingly supported the program because they thought that this was what was expected of them. In reality, I suspect that many of these supervisors saw training as taking their subordinates away from their day-to-day jobs; that is, it was a necessary evil, not an investment in their workforce.

The better approach is to think of employee development as a continuum from the time an employee enters on duty until the day he leaves the organization. After all, it's the employees who serve your customers, not the building, the computer system, or your manuals. Since that is the level where the rubber meets the road, this is where you need to make your largest investment and where you will get the biggest bang for the buck.

Along these lines, think of orientation as the point where training begins and then continues for the duration of each employee's career. Let's look at this life cycle a little more closely.

After orientation, the employee should receive a sufficient amount of training to ensure she will be able to independently perform her job. Depending upon the nature and complexity of the job, as well as the number of new hires/selectees, this may entail some combination of formal classroom training, reading assignments, and one-on-one mentoring and can take anywhere from several hours to a few years before the employee becomes a journeyman. Where possible, I recommend placing trainees in some form of a team or group environment, with a mentor or coach at their disposal, so that they will be able to develop in a positive and supportive environment.

I also recommend that trainees both be evaluated and receive solid feedback during this period. It is simply the right thing to do and will help you identify problems early on, rather than letting them fester and develop into bigger problems. Trainees both need and deserve to know how they are doing so that they can make any necessary adjustments. At the same time, if someone is struggling and looks like he is going to be a problem, better to address the situation early on, instead of scrambling near the end of or after the probationary period.

Once the trainees become journeymen, your obligation to train them does not end. As stated earlier, it continues throughout their career.

The best way to approach this is by first identifying the competencies required for your organization. Competencies are the skills and abilities needed by an organization so that it can successfully achieve its mission. If an organization starts out by identifying the competencies it would like to have in its "ideal state" and then compares them with the competencies that its employees actually have in the organization's "current state," the organization will know exactly where its gaps are and can plan accordingly.

I suggest this approach because it looks at training in a holistic manner. After all, the real concern is not how you develop your trainees; it is how you develop your entire workforce. In my experience, far too often, management tended to focus its training on the new people or to offer it when legislative and/or procedural changes were made or when there was a quality problem in a particular area. All of these are good reasons to give training. The problem with this approach is that it is ad hoc and piecemeal and is not really focused on any overall strategy. That is why I always come back to tracking competencies. If you look at the competencies your organization needs, compare them to what you have, and then try and bridge the gap, you will know exactly where your holes are and can plan your training accordingly.

Planning Your Training: A Competency Grid. A competency grid is simply a visual tool that compares a division, unit, and/or section's desired competencies with the actual competencies of each employee in that activity. Every employee works closely with her supervisor to assess her strengths and weaknesses in each competency, and these assessments are then listed on the grid for all to see. The activity's training plan is then designed to bridge these gaps, making training much fairer and more transparent than what the employees have been used to.

This is an example of a simple competency grid:

Figure 6-1. Sample Competency Grid

Employee Name	Competency A	Competency B	Competency C	Competency D	Competency E
John Doe	Expert	Expert	Expert	Journeyman	Expert
Jane Doe	Expert	Expert	Journeyman	Expert	Journeyman
John Smith	Journeyman	Journeyman	Journeyman	Journeyman	Novice
Fred Brown	Journeyman	Journeyman	Expert	Novice	Novice
Mary Davis	Novice	Novice	Novice	Novice	Novice
Ideal State	2 E's, 3 J's	3 E's, 2J's	2 E's, 3 J's	2 E's, 1J	1 E, 3 J's
Current State	2 E's, 2 J's, 1 N	2 E's, 2 J's, 1 N	2 E's, 2 J's, 1 N	1E, 2 J's, 2 N's	1 E, 1 J, 3 N's
Gap	1 J	1 E,	1 J	1 E	2 J's

Training Plan:

Competency A—pair Mary Davis with John Doe twice a week for one hour to make her proficient in that competency

Competency B—consult with John Smith and Fred Brown and determine which of them should take a one-week advanced class on this topic in Baltimore, MD

Competency C, D, and E—same approach

Priorities:

Plan:

As you can see, this grid clearly shows where the activity's primary training needs are, so it becomes easier to decide whom you should send for training and why. You might even want to consider color-coding each box to make it even easier to view (e.g., green for expert, yellow for journeyman, and red for novice).

I recommend that this grid be posted within each activity and that the employees be involved in the actual analysis of the needs, the prioritization of the needs, and the development of the training plan. In this way, everyone will feel a part of the process, and the typical complaints about favoritism will evaporate because the employees will have had the chance to participate and it will be an open process.

I also suggest that when you hold your periodic performance feedback meetings with your employees (optimally, much more than twice a year), you use that occasion to talk to them about their development and how they are doing in improving their competencies. In this way, you will make employee development a regular part of the discussion, rather than the off-the-cuff conversation that it usually is.

Managing Performance with Individual Development Plans. Many organizations use individual development plans (IDPs) as a way to develop their employees, and that can be a good thing. The problem I have seen is that a lot of work is initially put into writing up impressive sounding plans, but then little follow-up ever seems to take place. My advice is to put together IDPs only if you truly plan to use them as intended.

Perhaps the best way to use IDPs is in the manner I just described. Require that the IDP be discussed whenever the employee receives prescheduled performance feedback. In fact, I encourage organizations to add a block on the employee appraisal form that requires the initials of both the supervisor and the employee acknowledging that the employee's IDP was addressed during the performance feedback session.

Mandatory Training. Another related component of employee development is what I call mandatory training. This is training that does not necessarily relate directly to the team's competencies but that is still required by the national, state, or local organization. This training may concern techniques for preventing sexual harassment, information technology security, employee safety and health issues, or other topics.

In many cases, these classes are required in response to an incident that has caused the organization embarrassment and/or put it at risk in some fashion. For example, women at one or more sites may have been sexually harassed, or there could have been a serious breach in the organization's information security system. Whatever the reason, the training usually occurs after the event has generated enough adverse publicity that a senior official in the organization decides to respond by requiring that every employee take a class that theoretically prevents the incident(s) from recurring.

The problem with some of these classes is that they tend to become a part of the organization's annual training program, even if they have outlived their usefulness. However, if they are required, management must comply, so the supervisor needs to ensure that every employee attends each mandated course. This can be easily tracked by adding additional columns onto the competency grid, by developing a separate grid, or simply maintaining a spreadsheet. The important thing here is to plan for the training at the beginning of the year and to then get it done.

Developing Your Supervisors

An important area that should require your attention is supervisory development. Supervisors are the lifeblood of any organization, and they must be carefully developed. That statement has never been truer than today, with the retirement of the

Class of '73, the lack of HR expertise, the increasing complexity of the work, and the increasingly litigious workforce.

To address this, I would take the same basic approach that I suggested for addressing your competencies: Identify and analyze both the ideal state and the current situation, and then develop a plan to bridge the gaps. Any such plan should involve developing a cadre of high-potential future supervisors (so you don't have to train every new supervisor from scratch), as well as your first- and second-line supervisors, your midlevel managers, and your current and future leaders.

The plan should recognize that supervisors, who directly oversee their subordinates, need different skill sets from managers, who manage through other supervisors; and that leaders require different skill sets from managers, since leaders focus more on establishing and advocating a vision, improving systems, and looking down the road.

The idea here is that there is a continuum through which supervisors pass as they move up through the organization, and that path should be as smooth as possible. The best way to accomplish this is through careful planning and early identification of your future stars and then following that up with constant development, using a wide range of tools, including an IDP, training classes, mentors, increasingly challenging assignments, reading material, and management development programs. I encourage you to ensure that at least some of these activities include interaction with experts from outside government if for no other reason than to ensure that future supervisors get exposed to as many ideas and approaches as possible.

I'm confident that if you make a heavy investment in your current and future management team, you will reap dividends in the years to come.

CHAPTER 7

Managing Performance and Accountability

It wouldn't surprise me if this were the section of the book that you are most interested in.[1] After all, whenever I speak to government managers about improving performance, they all want to know how they can hold their employees accountable. To do this, I think it is best if we first think in terms of roles and responsibilities, second about the performance management system itself, and third in terms of implementation of the system.

With respect to roles, every government manager needs to provide his employees with the training, tools, and expectations required so that they will both know what they need to do to succeed and be able to meet the requirements of the job. In other words, it is up to each employee's supervisor to put her in a position where she can properly perform her job. This means not only setting up the training and ensuring the employee has a decent work space, access to the computer system, a copy of the code of conduct, and appropriate performance standards but also addressing any problems that might develop along the way (e.g., running organizational interference if technical problems develop, providing the employee with additional training or guidance if they struggle in a particular area).

The employee is responsible for coming to work, learning as much as possible, and preparing to become a journeyman employee. Her job is not to be a passive participant in the training phase; it is to be an active player. Therefore, if she believes that she is not receiving proper training or the right tools, she needs to let management know what the problems are and try to work together to find an appropriate solution.

The Performance Appraisal System

Now that everyone's roles are clear, let's turn our attention to the performance appraisal system. There are two key components: (1) the employee's performance plan, which consists of the employee's performance standards; and (2) then administering the system. We'll cover the second area in the next chapter. Let's look at each in more detail.

The Employee's Performance Plan

The employee's performance plan is part of the government's overall performance appraisal system. In order to understand the system and how the performance plan fits within it, there are some key definitions that you should be aware of.

Critical element means a work assignment or responsibility of such importance that unacceptable performance on the element would result in a determination that an employee's overall performance is unacceptable. Such elements shall be used to measure performance only at the individual level.

Noncritical element means a dimension or aspect of individual, team, or organizational performance, exclusive of a critical element, that is used in assigning a summary level. Such elements may include, but are not limited to, objectives, goals, program plans, work plans, and other means of expressing expected performance.

Performance rating means the written, or otherwise recorded, appraisal of performance compared to the performance standard(s) for each critical and noncritical element on which there has been an opportunity to perform for the minimum period.

Performance standard means the management-approved expression of the performance threshold(s), requirement(s), or expectation(s) that must be met to be appraised at a particular level of performance. A performance standard may include, but is not limited to, quality, quantity, timeliness, and manner of performance.

Progress review means communicating with the employee about performance compared to the performance standards of critical and noncritical elements.[2]

Writing Performance Standards

The key component of the appraisal plan is the performance standards, since they serve as the basis for measuring the performance of the employees. First and foremost, the standards need to be aligned with your organizational goals so that everyone is concentrating on achieving the same objectives. If these are not aligned, people will focus on all sorts of things that may not be in the organization's best interests. Moreover, you may even find yourself in the uncomfortable position of having most, if not all, of your employees far exceeding their standards even as the organization fails to achieve its goals. This can happen if your organizational energy is diffused.

To me, a good visual analogy is the Death Star that was featured in the *Star Wars* movies.[3] The Death Star was a round, planet-size machine that was capable of destroying another planet. When the Death Star became operational, all of the energy forces in the machine came together in one focused laser beam that produced an enormous amount of focused energy and ultimately destroyed another planet.

Figure 7-1. Align Your Forces Like the Death Star

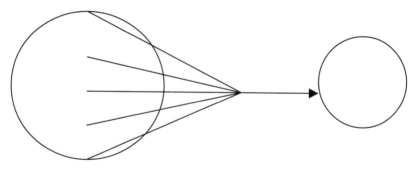

That is exactly what you want your performance standards to do: Ensure that all of your organizational energy is focused in a laser-like manner to achieve your organization's performance goals. When that doesn't happen, you wind up with a lot of wasted energy and employees working in an inefficient manner.

To provide a real-world example, I recall working with an organization that was responsible for conducting certain types of investigations. It was clear to me that senior management wanted to produce a high-quality product, yet it didn't measure the individual quality of its investigators. When managers started looking at the overall quality of the work being performed on a national basis, they quickly discovered that the quality of the investigations varied greatly by employee, in part because the performance standards sent a message that quality was not important and that employees would not be held accountable for poor quality. As a result, there was an enormous amount of rework going on. Management learned from this experience that if it wanted to consistently deliver a quality product, it needed to measure each employee's accuracy and ensure that everyone was focused on the same things.

Performance standards are very hard to write, and supervisors often have a difficult time objectively appraising their subordinates. What usually happens is that supervisors follow the path of least resistance and write standards that are so vague and/or so generic that (1) the employee doesn't really know what is expected of him; and (2) there is no real way to hold the employee accountable for poor performance because the standards do not specify what the employee is supposed to do in order to be considered fully successful.

Let's look at several examples of typical standards that I have seen and analyze how they play out in the workplace.

Element: Writes reports and management studies on topics assigned

Standard: Reports are accurate and well written and are generally submitted on a timely basis. Recommendations contained in the studies are based on sound logic and supported by the appropriate facts.

Analysis: This type of standard is so vague that it is virtually impossible to appraise someone against it. As a result, the supervisor simply uses her judgment to decide how the employee is doing. Although some supervisors probably like that since it provides them with in their minds maximum flexibility, it (1) is unfair to the employee, because he never really has anything to go by in determining how he is doing; (2) places the supervisor in an awkward position if she wants to take action against a poor employee; and (3) provides no real basis for making distinctions between employees. With this type of standard, little documentation about employee performance is ever maintained and no one, especially the supervisor, looks forward to the end of the appraisal period because everyone recognizes that each employee's appraisal will be based more on gut than on fact.

Element: Processes fiscal transactions

Standard: Processes a reasonable number of transactions per day with acceptable quality. Transactions containing errors are corrected within forty-eight hours.

Analysis: This standard is extremely vague. For example, what is a reasonable number of transactions per day? What is acceptable quality? How is it measured? The only real metric here involves correcting transactions within forty-eight hours, but how will that be measured, and how long is the employee expected to take to process fiscal transactions?

Element: Cooperation and organizational support

Standard: Serves as a team player and assists others when required. No more than three legitimate complaints will be received regarding the way the employee works with others and supports the organization.

Analysis: To me, as written this standard is very imprecise, to a large extent measures conduct, not performance, and tracks exceptions rather than day-to-day interactions. Moreover, how does one determine what a legitimate complaint is, since there is no real benchmark?

How does one go about writing solid and actionable performance standards? In my view, you need to write them in a way that allows you to determine how well each employee is actually doing his job and be able to make meaningful distinctions between people (i.e., who is doing an outstanding job, who is doing a satisfactory job, and who is doing a poor job). A good way to tell if you are on the right track is to compare your employees' appraisals relative to the performance standards and then see how they match your gut. What I mean is that most people know who the best and worst performers are in an organization. That is never a secret. If the standards you put in place generally result in the people you believe are your best receiving high ratings and the ones you think are the weakest receiving relatively low ratings, you are probably at least off to a good start.

Try to write the standards using the SMART principles that were described in Chapter 5 when I talked about the development of organizational metrics. The more your standards are specific, measurable, and attainable, the more actionable they will be and the more credibility they will have with the employees, which is very important.

Think of the overall performance plan and the standards themselves as part of a mini–balanced scorecard for each employee; in other words, they should be a system for measuring everyone's overall contribution. To do this, try to incorporate metrics that, where possible, at least track each employee's accuracy, output, timeliness, and customer satisfaction.

This, of course, is easier said than done, since you need to find a way to easily capture this information. I suspect that at least some of this information is probably in your computer system (e.g., individual output and/or timeliness may be easily measurable if each employee is responsible for a specific product or output). If not, you can either try to build fields for this in your system, assign each employee a specific code or number and capture the work that way, or have each employee record what he completes in a centralized database that is subject to supervisory verification.

Employee Output. With respect to employee output, you should count the number of widgets that each employee completes (assuming that the job in question can realistically be measured in this way). However, if the employee completes different types of outputs, you should consider assigning a weight to each type of work so that every employee's output is adjusted by the degree of difficulty of the work (e.g., end product A might be worth two standard man-hours, two points, two credits, two cases, or some other common measure; end product B might be worth four standard man-hours or points, and so on). In this way you can compare "apples to apples"; that is, you can measure the true output of each employee who performs the same type of work, regardless of the mix of their work.

In setting up a system to measure employee productivity, you need to determine what outputs will be measured; what their weights are, if any; what time, if any, will be excluded from the measurement period;[4] what is the minimum level of productivity that will be accepted; and how you will capture the data.

This is an extremely important and sensitive measure because if too much output is expected of the employees, they will find shortcuts for achieving the standard, and quality will suffer. Conversely, if too little productivity is expected, the organization's overall performance will decline because you will not be efficiently using your available resources.

Timeliness. Concerning timeliness, you need to know how long it takes an employee to produce a specific product or deliver a particular service. After all, your customers expect you to serve them as quickly as possible, and timeliness is always an important measure of your organization's overall delivery of service. That is why you should try to set up your computer system so that it can track work from the time it is assigned to an employee until the time it is completed. Be clear as to exactly what you will be measuring (e.g., from the beginning of a certain point in the process until the end of another point) and what the minimum acceptable level of timeliness is. In this way, there will be no surprises and no secrets, and you will know exactly how long it is taking each employee to complete their work.

Accuracy. Accuracy can surely be measured as long as you do a random sample of each employee's work and retain the review sheets for your records. To do this properly, I recommend that you identify what will be measured for accuracy, the criteria that will be used, the amount of work to be reviewed, the frequency of the reviews, the manner in which an employee can contest a negative quality determination, and the minimum level of acceptable quality. I would also record this information

in a database so that it can easily be retrieved and you can identify any patterns that require correction.

Customer Satisfaction. Very few government organizations
measure individual employee customer satisfaction. To some
extent, that makes sense, because you don't want to conduct
surveys of the public asking how each government employee is
doing. First of all, the public generally doesn't know what each
government employee does; second, even if they did, it would
be cost prohibitive to conduct such surveys.

That having been said, you may want to consider conducting surveys of stakeholders that frequently interact with your
employees. This will provide a good sense of how each employee is dealing with people from outside the immediate organization. It will also help drive the right behavior because once
employees know that the way they treat stakeholders will be
evaluated, they will be much more likely to exhibit the right
behavior, or pay the price with a lowered appraisal or adverse
award determination.

The same approach could also be taken for the service that
each employee provides to his internal customers. If an employee also knows that his internal customers will evaluate the
way he works with them, he will be even more likely to act
appropriately.

I suggest that you use a modified 360-degree review[5] of each
employee to measure the way he provides service to his customers. Such an approach provides a more in-depth and fair review
of each employee's overall performance, since many more people contribute to the evaluation than just the first-line supervisor. To me, this makes much more sense than basing the

evaluation of the employee's performance on merely the supervisor's judgment and perhaps a few "valid complaints."

Such an approach can be a bit tricky, however, if co-workers are asked to do the reviews. They may be uncomfortable participating in such a review if it can result in the subject of the review being fired or affect her pay. That is why I do not recommend including co-workers in this process.

Another approach is to make this element noncritical, meaning the employee cannot be fired for failure to meet the minimum expected level of performance. This may reduce the concerns that could arise from these reviews.

Regardless of the way you set up the standard(s) for this element, make sure that everyone understands the rules, the expectations, and how frequently such surveys will occur. Note I recommend that surveys be administered at least twice a year and be averaged or weighted accordingly in order to give each employee the opportunity to improve.

The elements I have described are not all-inclusive; you can certainly add other ones if they make sense for your organization. However, I am recommending that, where possible, you include the four categories I just described because they provide you with a fair and well-balanced view of each employee's performance, which is one of the key goals of a performance appraisal system.

In terms of writing the actual standards, let's take the three examples I provided earlier and see if we can make them more meaningful and precise and more consistent with the SMART principles.

Element: Writes reports and management studies on topics assigned

Standard: A minimum of 85 percent of reports are submitted by the due date. Reports are accurate at least 85 percent of the time. Any required changes are submitted within two days 90 percent of the time.

Analysis: This standard is much more accurate and precise than the earlier one and lets the employee know exactly what is required to meet the minimum level of acceptable performance. Now you might be thinking to yourself that this is all well and good, but how will I ever track all of these reports and be able to accurately recall what the employee's performance was in this particular category? My response is that such a thought indicates you have a problem in terms of how you are tracking your employee's performance. However, don't feel too bad, because I believe most supervisors have the same problem.

In order to address that issue, I recommend you design a simple one-page review sheet (see Figure 7-2.) that provides the employee with written and timely feedback on each report submitted, which you can retain in your employee file and refer to whenever you need to provide performance feedback (e.g., on the annual appraisal, during the mid-year review, or during any other feedback session).

Element: Processes fiscal transactions

Standard: Processes at least sixty transactions a day with an accuracy rate of at least 92 percent. At least 85 percent of transactions are processed within five days of receipt, and 95 percent of erroneous transactions are processed within two business days.

Analysis: This standard is much tighter and clearer than the original example I provided. Note that the number of fiscal transactions processed per employee should be rel-

Figure 7-2. Employee Review Sheet

Employee Name _____ Date_____

Report _____ Date Assigned _____

Date Due _____ Date Received _____ Timely Y __ N __

Accuracy of Report

Facts are Correct Y __ N __ If not, explain why

_____

_____

Conclusions are well documented Y __ N __ If not, explain why

_____

_____

Report is well written Y __ N __ If not, explain why

_____

_____

Date report to be resubmitted by _____ Date report received _____

Report resubmitted within two days? Y __ N __

Other comments _____

_____

_____

_____   _____
Signature of reviewing official   Signature of employee

_____   _____
Date   Date

atively easy to track through the computer system. Moreover, for the purpose of this example, I am assuming that most transactions are relatively similar in complexity, so I am not assigning a different weight to each type of transaction. Although a few transactions are probably more difficult than the others, I am also assuming that everyone has a relatively similar work mix, and that the number of sixty transactions per day takes that mix into account.

Regarding timeliness, that too should be relatively easy to track in the computer system by employee, especially if you set up those parameters beforehand. Concerning accuracy, using a review sheet like the one in Figure 7-2 (without the references to timeliness) should suffice to track the quality of each person's work.

Element: Cooperation and organizational support

Standard: Serves as a team player and assists others when required. Employee receives a score of at least 75 or higher on his modified 360-degree review. No more than three legitimate complaints will be received regarding the way the employee works with others and supports the organization (a legitimate complaint is an allegation that the employee did not appropriately serve the team, another member of the organization, a customer, or a stakeholder in a manner that was consistent with the organization's core values and one that has been verified as being accurate by a member of management).

Analysis: By incorporating the modified 360-degree review, you have put in place a reliable way to measure how well the employee has both cooperated with and supported the organization. Moreover, because it is the sum total of the observations of a number of people, it is much more difficult for the employee to allege supervisory bias. Finally, since you have defined what constitutes a legitimate complaint, everyone knows what the criteria are, making it much easier to hold the employee accountable.

There are a couple of other approaches you should be aware that will make your standards even better. First of all, when an element contains several performance standards (such as the examples I gave for writing reports or processing fiscal transactions), it is important to indicate how the employee will be rated if she meets some but not all of the standards. In other words, if she meets two out of the three standards (say, timeliness and productivity) but not the third (accuracy), has she met the element or failed it? You need to be clear about this point. Are any of the standards more important than the others? Be clear regarding this as well.

Second, note that I incorporated several key components (timeliness, productivity, accuracy) into the elements because, in my example, the employee would have had more than one distinct task (i.e., writing reports, processing fiscal transactions). However, if the employee has one primary task (e.g., processing claims, servicing loans, rehabilitating customers, repairing machines, making decisions), then you could have one element devoted to productivity, one to timeliness, one to accuracy.

The point here is that there is more than one way to do this. The key is to design your standards in a way that makes sense for each job, and the best way to do that is to make the standards as simple, measurable, fair, and accurate as you can.

Third, recognize that every job is not so easy to measure and that some components of certain jobs may be close to impossible to assess. For example, it might be pretty tough to precisely measure what a research scientist does on an annual basis. Be aware that there is no governmentwide requirement that each aspect of every job be measured numerically. Sometimes you have to use a more generic measure. However, where possible, it is generally better to have standards to which you can assign numbers.

Another approach that I strongly recommend is to articulate at least two levels of performance for each standard: the minimally acceptable level and the far-exceeds level. The reason I advocate this approach is that it lets everyone in advance know what the rules are, so when it comes time to distribute rewards people already know how they are doing and whether or not they will receive an award.

To be fair, some people will disagree with this approach because they feel it reduces their flexibility, and, to some extent, that is true. However, I think that is part of the problem and why I advocate a more rigid approach. In my experience, government supervisors often give awards to the people they like and not necessarily to the people who are making the most important contributions. Such an approach tends to undermine the employees' faith in management and its decisions, because employees learn that you get rewarded on the basis of whom you know instead of on what you do.

By establishing in advance the criteria required to receive an award, you set up a methodology whereby people are reliably rewarded for excellent performance and employees whose performance is merely average or worse will not receive an award. That having been said, there will still be plenty of room for flexibility because every employee who far exceeds his standards doesn't have to receive the same amount of money. However, I would ensure that if someone's performance exceeds the standard by 50 percent, he should receive more than another person who exceeds it by 25 percent. In addition, management should retain the right to give out awards for special acts or contributions. The point here is that employees need to see a clear relationship between the performance appraisal process and rewards and recognition. There is more on this subject in Chapter 9.

CHAPTER 8

Follow-Up on Accountability: Administering the Appraisal System

It is one thing to develop a solid set of performance standards but quite another to successfully implement it. In my experience, one of the biggest problems, if not the biggest, with performance management in government is the lack of follow-up by supervisors. This often dictates whether the organization is successful in managing its employees' performance

Whenever I speak to or work with government organizations, I constantly hear that this is one area where almost everyone struggles. Whether that is the result of a lack of knowledge, limited time, a culture that moves problem employees around, weak support from upper management, or some other factor, poor performance must and can be dealt with if the organization has the will and the skill. There are specific ways to administer the appraisal system to improve performance management in your organization, so let's talk about how to do just that.

First of all, if you do not have good standards, follow the advice I provided in Chapter 7 and develop them. Include the employees and the union, if you have one, in the process, since transparency will improve the credibility of the standards. Carefully listen to their comments, criticisms, and suggestions, since it is better to be aware of these concerns early on and address them at that time if necessary, rather than have to deal with them when you are before a third party.

Managing the Individual Employee

Assuming you have provided the employee with the training, tools, and expectations (discussed in Chapter 6) and have developed the requisite performance standards, the next and most important step is to manage each employee's performance. Simply put, the key here is communication—tracking how everyone is doing and then giving employees fair and frequent feedback.

Unfortunately, many if not most government supervisors spend relatively little time and energy talking with the employees about their performance, which often leaves the employees unsure about how they are doing and gives them the impression that their boss is not particularly interested in them.

The little time that supervisors and employees spend together discussing individual performance goes something like this: During April (the midpoint of the appraisal period), the supervisor has a brief conversation with each employee and tells him that he is "doing fine." The supervisor asks no questions and then quickly presents the employee with the appraisal form to review, letting the employee know that she is in a hurry and has to meet with the next employee. Invariably, the form contains a box that has been checked by the supervisor indicating that the employee is performing at the fully successful level; there are no comments anywhere. She then asks the employee to sign the form, which he dutifully does. That ends the discussion about the employee's performance, and another one does not take place until six months later, when the appraisal period ends.

At the end of the appraisal period, both the supervisor and the employee start to become a bit uncomfortable. From the employee's perspective, he has received virtually no feedback throughout the year regarding his performance. He is reasonably certain that he will not be fired because no one ever seems to get fired; by the same token, he has no idea whether he will be rated "outstanding," "highly successful," or "fully successful."[1]

From the supervisor's point of view, she has to rate a large number of people to whom she has given virtually no feedback during the year. Moreover, she has to decide how to appraise employees against performance standards that are very vague. What usually happens is that she sits down with her supervisor(s) in a room behind closed doors, and they decide by gut the level at which each employee will be rated. The criteria are, of course, questionable, to say the least, and the people whom management likes the most wind up with the highest ratings, even though there is no factual basis to support these determinations.

The supervisor leaves this meeting knowing that there is strength in having upper-level management support her ratings but also with a knot in her stomach because she now has to explain the rationale behind each rating to her subordinates. She then meets with each employee as required and tepidly presents

them with their ratings. If anyone receives a rating below outstanding and objects, she simply plays the role of the victim by
implying that upper-level management made her do it and, if she
had her way, she would have rated the employee higher.

From the employee's perspective, he sees that appraisals are
less a function of what you do relative to the performance standards and more a function of whom you know and/or how well
you kiss up to management. In most cases, he will not want to
ruffle any feathers by filing a grievance or EEO complaint, but
he will privately sulk, most certainly complain to his co-workers,
and slowly but surely become cynical and at least somewhat
disaffected. Is this any way to run a government?

Fortunately, there is another way of managing employee
performance that will make everyone feel better and, more important, result in improved performance. The key, as I mentioned earlier, is communication, and by this I mean frequent,
honest, and, where necessary, detailed interactions between the
supervisor and the employee. Let's examine what I mean by
this.

The supervisor should be talking to the employee about his
performance much more frequently than twice a year. Employees need and deserve that feedback, and it is the right thing to
do. In addition, when you have to do something to the employee that could be viewed as a negative action (ranging from
a counseling letter, to a performance improvement plan, to giving the employee "only" a fully satisfactory rating, to not giving
the employee an incentive award),[2] it will always be received
better if the employee can see it coming, and the only way he
will see it coming is by having more frequent communication
that emphasizes what he can expect on the basis of his year-to-
date performance.

I recommend that supervisors communicate with their employees at least quarterly, although I think that monthly is even better. The communication doesn't always have to be a face-to-face meeting; it can simply be a written note and/or form that lets them know how they are doing relative to their standards (both the fully successful and the outstanding levels) and their peers. In this way, the employees know exactly how they are doing with respect to both retaining their job and achieving awards. There are no surprises and no secrets, and as long as the supervisor then appraises the employees according to the guidelines of the standards, every employee will be able to predict what his appraisal will be and whether he will receive an award. In other words, the system will become meaningful and credible to the employees because it will be reliably applied to them. I tried this exact approach in my last office, and employee satisfaction with this approach rose by more than twenty points because the employees saw that this was a system they could believe in.

A good way to communicate on a monthly basis is by giving employees a simple report card that provides the information I described two paragraphs ago. Such a card lets them know how they are doing and gives them the opportunity to raise any concerns they may have about the numbers. Moreover, it provides the supervisor with the opportunity to give the employee feedback ("great job, keep it up"; "you're doing just fine, thanks for all of the good work"; "I think you could do better, especially in quality, where your error rate is too high"; "if you don't increase your productivity by at least 1.5 widgets per day, I am going to have to officially give you a counseling letter"). The point here is that by issuing monthly report cards, you can give the employee immediate feedback and positively reinforce excellent performance or prod the employee to improve his performance when necessary.

This is an example of a monthly employee report card.

Figure 8-1. Sample Employee Report Card

	Employee Report Card			
Month	*Output*	*Accuracy*	*Timely (days)*	*Leave (hours)*
Oct	3.8 (82)	88%	14	0
Nov	4.0 (74)	90%	11	8
Dec	4.2 (77)	85%	17	11
Jan	3.9 (68)	100%	9	24
Feb	4.4 (87)	90%	15	0
March	3.9 (74)	92%	21	8
Your Average	4.0 (76)	93%	14.5	8.3
Team Average	3.8 (73)	88%	13	6.1
Successful	3.5	85%	15	N/A
Outstanding	4.0	92%	10	N/A

Note: Under output, I have listed both the average number of widgets completed per day as well as the total number for the month (in parenthesis), as they give a fuller picture of the employee's contribution. I have also listed attendance, even though that is not part of the employee's standards, in order to give a sense as to how often the employee was present during the period and contributing to the team.

As I have stated earlier, some positions are not that easy to measure, so monthly report cards probably won't work for them. Under those circumstances, quarterly conversations or a brief note letting the employee know how he is doing should suffice. The point here is that the better you communicate with your employees about how they are doing, the easier it will be for you to manage their performance.

Managing the Performance of Your Group

While managing the performance of each employee is extremely important, from the supervisor's perspective, managing the performance of the group is even more important. After all, the supervisor is evaluated on the basis of the performance of the group as a whole, not how each employee performs as an individual. Of course, to a large extent, the performance of the group is a function of the way the employees perform as individuals. However, the way they interact and work together as a team is what it is all about.

So how do you get the employees to work together as a team? First of all, remember the basic premise behind this book: If your systems are properly aligned, your employees will all focus on what is important to the organization, and this will bring a high degree of synergy. This means ensuring that people have the right training, tools, and expectations; making certain that the physical plant promotes a reasonable degree of interaction among the employees; and ensuring that the performance standards and rewards programs recognize both group and individual achievement. Second, you need to establish good communication between management and the employees and between the employees themselves, since that will also contribute to the group working as a team and not just as a bunch of individuals. Along these lines, I highly recommend that you hold a team meeting at least once a week, if not daily. The purpose of this meeting should be to discuss performance, share information, and gather everyone's perspective on the key issues confronting the team. In essence, the team's performance goals are the anchor for the team and what everyone should focus on.

I firmly believe in posting both individual and group performance on the team's bulletin board.[3] The idea behind this approach is to share virtually the same information with the employees that management has so that they feel more connected and more responsible for achieving the goals and objectives of the organization, instead of merely standing idly by and not getting involved.

That having been said, posting individual performance information generally works best when multiple members of the team have the same positions and performance standards and their jobs are relatively easy to measure. Under these circumstances, providing such information to the employees gives them a greater sense of context regarding how they are doing; demonstrates a high degree of transparency; prevents the supervisors from protecting their favorites and/or going after good performers that they don't like; and almost forces the organization to reliably treat all of their employees according to the numbers.

By the same token, such an approach normally prompts a high degree of internal discussion, as employees want to know why some people are doing much better than others. They quickly start to recognize that, to a large extent, overall performance is a function of the sum of its individual parts and try to pull up the weaker employees. In addition, people at the bottom of the performance spectrum will realize they can no longer hide and will make a concerted effort to improve as long as they are convinced that management is serious about dealing with poor performance.

Posting individual employee information can be controversial, since at least some people (usually the weakest employees) may feel that such an approach violates their privacy. In order to address this concern, I advocate posting the information anonymously, using a number or symbol, rather than a name, to identify each employee's performance. By taking such an approach, you allow everyone to see how she is doing and how each of her peers is performing, but she won't know whom the symbols represent. Of course, don't be surprised if the employees talk to each other and figure some of that information out;

however, that is between them. If they decide to share such information, everyone ultimately profits because you will have greater communication and significant upward peer pressure.

Here is an example of what posting individual performance within a team might look like:

Figure 8-2. Sample Posting of Individual Employee Performance Information

Individual Employee Performance				
Month: January Employee	*Output*	*Accuracy*	*Timely (days)*	*Hrs Absent*
A	4.3 (90)	86%	11	8
B	4.1 (83)	98%	14	14
C	4.1 (90)	88%	21	0
D	3.8 (72)	83%	17	24
E	3.5 (60)	85%	13	40
F	3.1 (67)	90%	18	3
Average	4.0 (77)	87%	13	15
Successful	3.5	85%	15	
Outstanding	4.0	92%	10	

Note: Under output, I have listed both the average number of widgets completed per day as well as the total number for the month (in parenthesis), as they give a fuller picture of the employee's contribution. I have also listed attendance, even though that is not part of the employee's standards, in order to give the team a sense as to how often each employee was present during the period and contributing to the team.

As you can see, this type of information provides the team with powerful information about how everyone is doing and lets team members identify individual gaps that they can address in order to improve the team's overall performance.

When I was detailed to another organization, I asked a section chief to try this concept within his area of jurisdiction. He agreed and reported back to me just two weeks later that he was amazed by the reaction. People started asking all sorts of questions, wanting to know what they could do to increase their performance, why some people were not pulling their weight, and so on. He was thrilled by the increased energy and focus and how it translated into improved performance within his team.

Dealing with Poor Performers

I covered this topic extensively in two of my previous books,[4] so I am not going to spend as much time on it here. The key to dealing with poor performance is to communicate with the employee and address it early and to make a good-faith effort to help her improve. If that doesn't work, you move to the formal stage (the Performance Improvement Plan, or PIP). Be firm but fair, apply the system as intended, and don't hope the problem will go away.

Addressing performance problems head-on is the only way to go; if you do that, everyone will get the message you are serious. Moreover, the employees themselves will resolve many of the performance issues once they realize that if they don't pick things up and improve, management will take action.

On the other hand, if you dillydally, people will not treat you seriously, which will then force you to spend a lot more of your precious time prodding the poor performers to step it up—and they won't. Remember, everyone watches what management does. If people see that management will not tolerate poor performance, the vast majority of employees will silently applaud you. The bottom 10 percent, naturally, will not, but they will take the message that they had better get cracking or they may be out of a job.

Firing poor performers is really not that difficult as long as you follow the process, try to assist the employee, and have good documentation. The burden of proof (substantial evidence) is relatively low, and management's success rate before third parties is relatively high (80–85%).

If you stay the course and treat everyone the same, you will do just fine.

A Note About the Supervisors

This book has focused on improving performance by managing through systems. The basic premise has been that if you have well-designed systems that are properly aligned and that work together, they will positively impact on the knowledge and culture of your organization, helping your employees to deliver the results that you are looking for.

That having been said, do not underestimate the importance of your supervisors in making these systems work properly. After all, in my experience, if you have good supervisors working with bad systems, they will eventually work together to try to improve those systems. Conversely, if you have bad supervisors working with good systems, they will eventually find ways to undermine the systems by not properly applying them, treating the employees in a disparate manner, and so on. That is why the supervisors are so crucial to an organization's success and why you need to focus so much of your attention on developing them and ensuring that they are implementing the systems as intended.

I recall earlier in my career giving what I thought were excellent speeches to the troops, only to later find out that some of the supervisors were telling their employees to disregard my remarks. In essence, their message was that I would be around for only a relatively short period of time, so the employees should listen to the supervisors and ignore me. I realized that unless the supervisors were on board with the direction I wanted to take the organization, they would be a major stumbling block in any change effort that I wanted to undertake.

I decided to spend quite a bit of time sharing my vision and values with the supervisors and bringing in outside experts to try to develop them. Some of them definitely came around and became change agents, while others did not and remained rooted in the past. Eventually, I concluded that I could not go forward with supervisors I did not trust and who were likely to be at odds with the direction I wanted to take the organization. As a result, I had to replace roughly half of the supervisors,[5] which was painful but, in retrospect, absolutely the right thing to do.

The point here is that if your organization is experiencing performance problems, the odds are that your supervisors are probably part of the problem. Some of them may simply be technicians who are in the wrong position; they may lack knowledge or experience; they may not be willing or capable of dealing with difficult people; or it may be a function of their attitude.

For example, I recall one supervisor who had a sign on his desk that said, "What part of 'no' don't you understand?" Not exactly a positive message, was it? Another supervisor was a nice person, but she was also a procrastinator and always had an excuse as to why she couldn't meet her goals. A third supervisor was strong and tough, but she treated the employees so harshly that no one wanted to work for her out of fear of incurring her wrath. Regardless of the reason, if your supervisors are contributing to your performance problems, you need to address this issue pronto.

My advice is to confront each of the supervisors you deem

to be a problem and be honest and straightforward with her. Let the supervisor know you consider her to be a problem, tell her why, and explain to her what she needs to do to improve. Make a good-faith effort to help her, and give her a reasonable amount of time to show she can meet your needs. If that doesn't work, deal with her as you would with any unsuccessful employee, and find someone else who can do the job.

Remember that your people system is one of your most important management systems because it impacts upon the folks who do the actual work of the organization—your employees. Since this system is so critical to your operation, it must be administered by competent and well-trained supervisors who have good attitudes and are willing to deal with difficult situations. In other words, if you are unhappy with them, either you change your supervisors, or you *change your supervisors.*

Holding employees accountable is one of the most important jobs of a supervisor. If you do this well, you will honor and recognize outstanding performance; let the successful people know that they are performing in an acceptable manner but also show them what they need to do to take things up a notch; and assist poor performers to improve. If all else fails, you will take appropriate action. If you develop these skills you will quickly see a noticeable improvement in your organization's performance. This will happen because the employees will finally believe that you are serious about performance management and that unacceptable performance is exactly that: unacceptable.

CHAPTER 9

The Rewards and Recognition and Renewal Systems

The rewards system is the pay and benefits structure but also includes incentives, celebrations, and informal rewards and recognitions. Given the fact that the government's pay and benefits structures are usually set by law, I am going to focus almost exclusively on the incentives, celebrations, and informal rewards and recognition components. First and foremost, you need to think about rewards and recognition as a system that reinforces excellent performance and behavior. It should not be used to reward people for merely doing their job and meeting the minimum standards of performance. Unfortunately, I've seen this happen far too often in government, when virtually every employee both receives and continues to expect to receive an award. Once that happens, the rewards program becomes watered down to the point where bonuses become meaningless, since employees expect to be rewarded automatically every year, regardless of what they have contributed to the organization. In essence, the bonuses simply become an extension of the employees' salaries, and they do not motivate employees to do better because they expect to be rewarded for simply doing their jobs.

Once this happens, the rewards program actually becomes a de-motivator, because the better employees see that they are receiving virtually the same amount of bonus money as the slackers and the malcontents. They begin to wonder why they should be killing themselves for the organization if they are going to be treated the same way as people who are just going through the motions or, even worse, pulling the organization down. Eventually, some of the top performers will look elsewhere for a job as they conclude that the organization is not serious about performance and they want to be associated with a winner. By the same token, other employees will begin to slow down, deciding that it is not worth striving to exceed their goals if they are going to receive the same bonus for simply performing at the acceptable level.

Under the very real scenario that I just described, the biggest loser is the organization, because its rewards program has driven out some of its best people and caused some of its better performers to slow down and underperform. Meanwhile, the middle 60 percent, 70 percent, or even 80 percent of the employees (i.e., the ones who don't rock the boat, perform acceptably, and watch what happens) begin to recognize that the rewards program is relatively meaningless and act accordingly. Conversely, the winners are the weakest employees, because they are left alone through benign neglect; yet they still receive bonuses and are allowed to continue to be the nattering nabobs of negativity they have always been.

Obviously, under this scenario, the rewards program is not working and for all intents and purposes has become a *disincentive awards program*. That, in a nutshell, is the problem with most government rewards and recognition programs. They simply don't do what they set out to do. As a result, what should be a positive program ultimately becomes a negative one and fosters frustration, cynicism, and sometimes downright anger and often results in a series of grievances and EEO complaints. I'm sure that many government managers would be happier if the program simply went away.

So why aren't most government rewards and recognition systems effective? First of all, the government usually does not set aside a lot of money in its awards pool, and a few hundred dollars in bonus money is not likely to get many people's attention. If the government were to pay thousands and thousands of dollars to its employees in bonuses (although it often does that for its senior executives), that might provide greater incentive to the employees, but it would also bring even more scrutiny and second-guessing from both the media and the public, so I don't think that is going to happen anytime soon, especially with the deficit climbing at an alarming pace.

Putting aside the amount of the awards pool, the government's rewards and recognition systems usually don't work well for two basic reasons: (1) they are not properly designed and aligned; and (2) they are not fairly and consistently implemented. Let's look at both issues more closely.

Design and Alignment

As I have emphasized throughout this book, an organization's management systems must be properly aligned in order to focus the organization's energy on its goals and objectives.

Given the fact that the rewards and recognition system can have a powerful positive or negative impact on the organization's performance, it is essential that the rewards system be properly aligned with the organization's goals and objectives and its other management systems.

Let me give you a few examples that I hope will reinforce this key point. Let's assume that your organization is committed to top-notch performance, including high quality. If you then reward people and/or teams that have high output but low quality, you will be sending a mixed message. After all, on one hand you will be preaching that quality is job one, while on the other hand you will be sending a message that output is what really matters and quality isn't that important. Such an approach will breed both cynicism and confusion, as people will conclude that the organization doesn't mean what it says and doesn't care about quality.

That exact scenario occurred in an organization I worked for. Our headquarters started hammering its field offices to improve productivity, but every now and then it would also murmur that quality was equally important. Everyone was skeptical about the importance of quality given the constant push to improve productivity and the infrequent after-the-fact references to quality. The general sense was that if the organization put its money where its mouth was and rewarded high quality in the same way it rewarded increased productivity, it would demonstrate that the organization was at least somewhat serious about producing a quality product. Lo and behold, at the end of the year, the field office that received the highest group award for performance (more than $400,000) had the second lowest quality in the nation! People were flabbergasted by this and quickly concluded that the organization's leadership was not serious about quality.

Once the leadership team became aware of the national reaction to its payout, it vowed to learn from its mistake and to realign its rewards decisions, which to its credit it did. However, the damage to its credibility was already done, and it never fully regained the trust of the field.

On another occasion, I recall working for an organization that claimed it was dedicated to working as a team. It brought in consultants to teach employees how to work together and placed a premium on group performance. However, the rewards system wound up being at odds with this objective, and this hampered performance.

The organization gave out only individual bonuses. As a result, the employees concluded that management was not really serious about teamwork, so most of them focused on performing their individual jobs and did not make much of an effort to assist their fellow employees; after all, for every minute they helped someone else, they were weakening their chances of getting an individual award.

In essence, the way that the rewards system was implemented wound up reducing teamwork, not supporting it; that is exactly why each and every design choice is so crucial.

The Elements of a Well-Designed System

By now, I hope you understand that your system must have a clear line of sight from the organization's goals to the program or field office level, on to the team level, and finally down to the individual. Such clarity ensures that everyone is focusing on accomplishing the same thing. This is the first element of a well-designed system.

Second, as stated earlier, your rewards system should work

together with your other systems and send the same message(s) to the employees.

The third component is that, for the most part, your awards criteria should be announced in advance so that everyone knows what she must do to receive a performance award (e.g., to achieve a bonus of $500, you must have a highly successful rating; to receive $1,000 you must have an outstanding rating; to achieve a far-exceeds rating in output, you must average ten widgets a day; to receive a far-exceeds rating in quality, your error rate must be no higher than 5 percent). In this way, every-one will know what the rules are and will be much more likely to strive for the level of performance that the organization is seeking.

Along these lines, you might consider breaking your re-wards criteria into chunks, such as quarterly intervals. I have found that annual rewards goals are often meaningless to em-ployees at the beginning of the rating period and that they don't begin to focus on them until the fourth quarter. To address this effect and to get them into the game from the get-go, I believe in establishing and announcing quarterly goals. In this way, for every goal they hit each quarter, they earn certificates, shares, or money that is paid out at the end of the quarter or fiscal year as appropriate. It simply makes the goals more immediate to everyone and keeps them focused.

The other approach is to make all of the decisions at the end of the appraisal period on the basis of a look back. I think you know how I feel about that.

I mentioned that most, but not all, of the award criteria should be announced in advance because you need to leave some flexibility to reward employees for special acts, such as one-time contributions over and above the call of duty that are worthy of recognition. These types of contributions are less predictable but are still important to the organization, so you need to set the right tone and reward unique contributions.

The fourth part of the plan should be to reward both group and individual contributions. As stated earlier, if you reward only individual contributions, people will be less likely to work together as they will want to focus on their individual performance. Conversely, if you reward only group achievement, employees may be less likely to strive to do their utmost as their focus will be on the group.

Remember, the group's performance is a function of both people working together and the sum of its individual parts. Also, you need to recognize that if you are going to have group rewards, you should announce in advance what the group has to do to receive awards, in the exact same way that you do for individual awards.

The fifth area of the plan is to establish a minimum level of conduct and performance that is expected of employees in order to qualify for most awards. After all, I would not want to give an award to someone who has been absent from work for most of the year, nor would I want to reward someone whose behavior has been unacceptable. On the other hand, while I believe that poor attendance should generally disqualify someone from receiving an annual group or individual award, it should not prevent people from receiving a one-time award for a special act if it is worthy of recognition.

Note that this last recommendation is unlikely to be supported by some unions, since in my experience many of them believe that performance and conduct are two separate issues. However, when it comes to awards, I think they are inextricably linked. After all, if someone's average performance is excellent, but the person is rarely at work or behaves inappropriately in other ways, I see no reason why that person should be rewarded. Furthermore, if the group achieves its goals but one of its members is on a performance improvement plan, it seems clear to me that this individual did not make a large enough contribution to the group to justify receiving an award.

The sixth part of the plan should be to include both nonmonetary and monetary awards. While money is clearly important, employees also crave recognition from their supervisors in the form of a "well done" note or a simple thank-you. Throughout my career, I constantly heard very good people complain that their supervisors didn't appreciate what they did for their organizations and that they didn't even acknowledge their contributions. Such treatment of employees rarely goes unnoticed, and it goes a long way toward fostering the perception that management does not care about them.

Now let me be clear about this; I am not advocating that supervisors thank employees for the sake of saying "thank you." That would water down the organization's drive for excellent performance and would send a mixed message to the employees. What I am saying is that supervisors should thank employees for their good work *whenever that is appropriate.* It lets employees know that we appreciate their efforts; it reinforces the right performance and behavior and doesn't cost anything. You might even say that thanking employees for the right reasons is one of the best investments that a supervisor can make.

Other forms of nonmonetary awards may include time off from work, recognition cards that acknowledge when an employee's actions embody one of the organization's core values, a parking space set aside for the employee of the month or quarter, an employee wall of fame showing the pictures of the top performers and telling their stories, a lottery card acknowledging a specific accomplishment,[1] or a bulletin board post with a picture of an employee and the customer she served and a description of how she helped that individual.

Celebrate Victories

I used to hold an annual employee breakfast for my employees. During this event, we showcased a variety of success stories and made sure that everyone was aware of the accomplishments of both the organization and its employees. I wanted the employees to know what we valued and why and to encourage as many people as possible to try to exceed our expectations. One year, I even showed a video that featured some of our employees highlighting what we had accomplished and letting people know where we were going. Years later, after we had achieved many of our objectives, I showed this video again so that our employees could see how much we had achieved and they could place their progress in its proper perspective.

Another form of celebration I learned to embrace was visits from other organizations. Once our office started receiving the attention of the outside world,[2] I started to use these visits as an opportunity to both celebrate and reinforce the outstanding performance, innovation, and creativity I was seeking to foster in our organization. Accordingly, whenever I gave visitors a tour of our office, I always took them to the desks of the employees who had made outstanding and/or unusual contributions and gave them the opportunity to speak and, ultimately, shine. After a while, other employees wanted to know what they had to do to be included on the tour. They were told that all they had to do was make an outstanding contribution like the other employees who were already featured on the tour. In this way, we were both celebrating success and encouraging other employees to also stand out.

Implementation

If you give me the choice between good systems and bad supervisors or bad systems and good supervisors, I will always choose the latter. This is because bad supervisors will eventually screw up good systems, while good supervisors will quickly recognize they have bad systems and will improve them; it's as simple as that.

Of course, the best-case scenario is to have good systems that are administered by good supervisors. When that happens, the rewards system takes on a degree of credibility that truly drives the organization's performance. Where appropriate and practicable, the supervisors work with the employees to establish the expectations early on in the appraisal year and notify them of the final goals and objectives; they provide the employees with periodic feedback on how they are doing relative to both the fully successful level and the level they need to achieve to receive awards; and they listen to employees when problems develop and try and make adjustments accordingly. In a sense, they work hand in hand to ensure a "win-win" situation for everybody. After all, if both the group and the individual employee achieve their goals, then the group and the employee should be rewarded, and the supervisor will obviously profit as well. It seems so simple, yet far too often things don't seem to work that way. Let's look at some of the reasons why that may happen and discuss strategies to address them.

Perhaps the surest way to frustrate everyone is to start the year with unrealistic goals that everyone knows are unattainable. When that happens, people tend to ignore the goals because they feel they are out of reach and not worth worrying about. The first reaction is that management is out of touch with reality and doesn't understand what the employees are dealing with. While that may indeed be the case, in my experience unrealistic goals are often driven by forces well above the local level, such as pressure from outside groups such as OMB, Congress, or stakeholders.

When that happens, you are unlikely to be able to change the goals. The one thing you can do is be honest and up front with your employees. Let them know where the goals came from and why and emphasize that you understand and share their frustration. Try to focus on improving a little each day, rather than worrying about how you will ever reach such unrealistic goals by the end of the performance cycle. Although you may not be able to achieve all of them, by letting the employees know that you are in this together, that you share their pain, and that you want to strive for incremental progress, you will keep them focused and may be able to mitigate some of their frustration over the unrealistic goals.

Another situation that often develops and frustrates employees to no end is the case in which a problem is discovered that prevents the employees from achieving their goals and management chooses to ignore it. When this happens, the employees take several messages: (1) management doesn't really care whether they achieve their goals or not; (2) management is not interested in listening to the employees and hearing their concerns; and (3) management is not willing to take the extra step to help the employees succeed. As you can imagine, if employees feel that way, it does not bode well for the organization.

For example, I recall a situation where an organization imposed a very tough productivity standard on its employees. The fully successful level was so challenging that most people gave up striving for the far-exceeds level. In fact, they became so worried about keeping their jobs that very few even thought about receiving awards.

The employees constantly complained about this to management and correctly pointed out that it was having an adverse impact on the organization's overall quality, but management held firm. Quality continued to plummet, and management finally relented and reduced its output expectations, but the damage had already been done, as the employees felt management cared only about themselves and not about the employees.

Perhaps the classic case of a poorly implemented government rewards and recognition system is the one in which there is no rhyme or reason why certain employees receive an award while others do not. In other words, there are no reliable consequences for outstanding performance. In my experience, this is what happens throughout most government organizations, and it drives both the employees and the union crazy, and sometimes the supervisors as well.

This occurs because the supervisors, generally out of good intentions, try to reward the people they think are most deserving. However, if there are no published criteria notifying people what they need to do to receive an award, little measurable data as to how people are doing relative to the organization's expectations, and little feedback to people about how they are doing, all you wind up with are highly subjective rewards determinations, and everyone knows that.

To complicate matters even further, supervisors are human and tend to have their favorites. They may spend a disproportionate amount of their time with some employees and even go to lunch with subordinates they feel comfortable with. As you might expect, a large percentage of the awards often goes to these folks. All this does, of course, is foster the perception that rewards are based more on personal relationships than on actual contributions to the organization, and before you know it you have a system that no one is happy with.

To throw one more monkey wrench into the mix, as we all know, supervisors always seem to face unusual situations, and special projects frequently come up for one reason or another. These may involve a sudden workload crisis, an issue that has caught the attention of the media, training a group of new employees, or something else. In most cases, the supervisors turn to the top 10 percent of their employees to handle these concerns and then look to recognize these employees for their accomplishments.

On one hand, this makes perfect sense, as most people would go to their strengths when the chips are down and then look to recognize those individuals for a job well done. On the other hand, by constantly giving these assignments to the top 10 percent, supervisors tend to create an "us versus them" mentality, giving the remaining employees the impression that only the cream of the crop will get the opportunity to earn rewards for special acts. It's a tricky situation for management because it wants to get the job done yet shouldn't want to create a caste system, either.

My advice is to assign only the most difficult and pressing situations to the top 10 percent and to give the other challenges and projects to the next one or two levels of your employees. In this way, the highest priorities will still be accomplished, but you will also begin to pull other people up into the elite group of employees and create a stronger base that you can turn to. Moreover, you will start to dilute the "us versus them" perception and provide more people with the opportunity to compete for awards. This, in turn, will help promote the sense that anyone who performs well may get the chance to work outside her normal position description and potentially receive an award.

Renewal

The renewal system is the way that organizations encourage and formalize continuous learning. For example, what structures or processes are in place for gathering together to learn or for sharing best practices? In my experience, government organizations tend to do pretty well in this arena, since they try to share best practices in a variety of different ways. For example, many, if not most, organizations hold both periodic team meetings and frequent conference calls with their area offices and/or headquarters during which they try and keep everyone in the loop, highlight successes, and promote new ways of doing business. Some even conduct monthly video conferences and/or webinars that allow for a greater degree of visibility and enable presenters to show slides or even videos. A large number of organizations also hold yearly conferences that allow people from all over the county, state, or country to meet face-to-face both as a group and/or one-on-one. All of these relatively formal approaches to learning are important and usually happen in government.

Another important way to promote learning is to look outside the organization for new ideas and new approaches. In my experience, sometimes the government does this well; other times it does not. This technique requires bringing in outside people who have new ideas, new approaches, and new perspectives and who are willing to challenge the mindset and "groupthink" that may have evolved within a particular organization.

For example, I was recently asked to work with a government organization that had a change of leadership. The career civil servants there were highly skeptical of me because they figured I would be the type of consultant who would swoop in, throw out a large number of radical ideas that were not grounded in reality, and then leave them to figure out how to implement my recommendations. Fortunately, they were willing to cut me a little more slack than most consultants because I at least had worked in the government for more than 30 years and knew their world.

Once I got there, I quickly provided them with a series of down-to-earth solutions for some of their most pressing HRM problems. This instantly gave me credibility with the senior leadership team, which in turn made employees even more open to my other ideas on such diverse areas as visual management, performance metrics, organizational structure, and the way leadership teams communicate with their employees, customers, and stakeholders. The point here is that once they became open to outside input and saw its potential benefits, they began to clamor for even more from me and other experts in their fields (e.g., experts in customer service, executive coaching, and employee surveys).

I'm always skeptical of organizations that never want to bring in outsiders. Invariably, the mindset is, "Why would we want to bring in someone who doesn't understand our organization, its history and its culture? After all, we have all the resources we need to solve our own problems." To me, this type of thinking is an indication that the organization has become too inbred and is becoming less and less open to new ideas. When this happens, it means that the organization is starting to develop blinders and is likely to miss out on vital opportunities to renew itself.

I remember early in my career when our headquarters wanted to detail me to another office so that I could learn from the experiences of people at that location. Our local management saw no reason to do this, so I didn't get to visit that office for months. When I finally got there, I quickly realized that it had much to offer, and I soaked up every bit of wisdom I could. For the rest of my career, I remained attached to that organization, recognizing that it was always there to both teach and support me.

The same type of mindset can also develop if the organization always promotes from within. Although promoting from within is very important, as it enables the organization to bring along its future stars and reward people who have devoted their time and energy to the organization, organizations also need to periodically bring in new blood, not just at the entry level but at higher levels. They need to do this for the same reason they should periodically bring in consultants or outside observers: to ensure that they are getting fresh ideas and new perspectives and to have at least some people question why things are being done the way they have always been done. Without a periodic stream of newcomers, organizations tend to stagnate.

An alternative to bringing outsiders into the organization is to go out and visit other organizations. I have found this to be an excellent way to learn what is going on in the world, meet new people, and watch different organizations in action. It's amazing what you can pick up by visiting a new organization. You will see another physical plant, a different workforce, and perhaps a unique way of doing things, and you will be able to converse with people who are probably coping with many of the same problems you are. I suspect you will find such a visit to be invigorating because you will probably pick up a few new things and will also take comfort in knowing that other people are trying to deal with the same challenges you are facing.

Another superb way to promote learning is to have a series of key employees attend one or more of the wide range of conferences that the government, its stakeholders, and the private sector offer each year. By this I mean conferences beyond those offered by the organization's headquarters or its area offices that relate either directly or indirectly to the mission of the organization. Such conferences include but are certainly not limited to the Excellence in Government Conference sponsored by *Government Executive* magazine, the American Society for Training and Development Conference; the Society for Human Resources Management Conference; the Federal Manager's Association Conference; the Federally Employed Women's Conference; the Blacks in Government Conference; the Open Government and Innovations Conference; the Annual Government Financial Management Conference; and similar meetings.

Organizations that send their people to these types of conferences will find that employees often bring back new ideas and different approaches, get a sense of what is coming down the road so they can get ahead of the curve, and get to mingle with and meet employees from other organizations. Building new relationships is crucial because it strengthens the attendees' networks and provides them with additional resources they can turn to when looking for new approaches or just someone they can bounce ideas off of.

For example, one of my former employees attended a conference and met a number of people he had previously heard of but had never met. For the first time, he was able to associate a face with the name. He built relationships with many of these individuals, which enabled him to call them whenever he needed help or needed to know where to turn for information.

Unfortunately, some organizations do not like to send their employees to conferences because of the cost factor and/or because they do not like having them away from the job site for too long. These are always considerations, but I encourage every organization to invest in its employees by at least occasionally sending them to outside conferences. If they don't, in the long run they will find they are being penny-wise and pound-foolish.

An easy and low-cost way of promoting learning is to have your employees read books and articles. While this requires an investment of both time and energy on the part of the employees and some bulk purchases by management, it ensures that the employees periodically take a step back and think and challenges them to consider some of their deeply held beliefs, perhaps growing in the process. A good way to reinforce this approach is to have brown-bag lunches where people who have read the books get together and discuss the contents. This provides the employees with an excellent forum for debating new ideas and finding ways to implement those that pass muster.

I recommend that the books and articles your employees

read cover a wide range of topics and not be limited to just business books and books about the government. There is enormous value in learning about many topics, including the arts, the sciences, spirituality, and self-help.

Another great source of information is biographies. I have learned an enormous amount by studying the lives of successful people. Reading about John Adams, Abraham Lincoln, Ulysses S. Grant, Harry Truman, Albert Einstein, Martin Luther King, Rembrandt, Steven Spielberg, and many, many others has taught me the value of believing in yourself and the importance of hard work, the need for continuous learning, and, most of all, the importance of persistence in the face of adversity. All of these lessons can and should be applied to government (and private sector) organizations and will help them continue to grow and evolve successfully.

A good way to track your organization's development and determine when you have a particular need for renewal is to conduct one or more internal surveys of your organization. These may include an annual employee satisfaction survey, an employee engagement survey, or a climate survey. If you do one or more of these surveys on an annual basis, they will provide you with a baseline estimate of how the employees and the organization are doing and where there are opportunities for improvement.

For example, I recall one year when our survey showed our employees were not as well connected to our customers as we would have liked, so we spent a lot of time trying to sensitize them to our clients' needs. We brought in customers to talk about their personal experiences and their interactions with our organization, and it made a big impact on our folks and ultimately made our organization better. The point here is that these surveys provide you with critical data that should be part of your renewal process.

Innovation and Creativity

Another way to ensure that your organization renews itself is to promote innovation and creativity. That sounds simple enough, but it is a lot more complicated than you might think. For example, large government bureaucracies are full of people who tend to be very protective of their turf. That is because there is only so far you can go in government and only so much money you can make, so turf becomes very precious to people. Therefore, when innovative changes are proposed that affect people's turf or the existing power structure, many employees push back either actively or passively in order to maintain the status quo. As multiple pushbacks occur and people give all sorts of reasons why change should not happen, many promising innovations die of benign neglect.

Another reason that innovation and creativity in government are often stifled is that governments usually have multiple field offices. In this situation, you want to preserve a reasonable degree of uniformity and consistency, because you want each office to deliver the same product and/or service with roughly the same degree of quality, timeliness, output, and customer satisfaction. Accordingly, you cannot allow each office to do its own thing; if you do, you are likely to have wide variances in performance. That is why larger organizations have all sorts of internal guides and manuals—to ensure that everyone takes the same basic approach, which, one hopes, has been time-tested and determined to be the most effective and efficient way of performing the work. When there is a lot of disparity between offices, the saying goes something like this: "When you have seen one office, you have seen one office."

On the other hand, if everyone is doing things the exact same way, over time, the mindset becomes "that is the way we have always done things," and people stop looking for new ways to get the job done. When that happens, the organization tends to become stagnant and does not take advantage of new ideas, technologies, methods, and approaches. Before you know it, the innovative people become frustrated, stop making suggestions, and ultimately leave. Eventually, the organization starts to slowly but surely lose ground to other more innovative organizations, and it develops a reputation of one that is living in the past.

To me, the best way to manage the contradictory goals of innovation and creativity *and* uniformity and consistency is to strike a balance between the two. On the creativity side, make sure that the organization has people in power who are open to new ideas. Periodically rotate people through committees that review projects, proposals, new ideas, and concepts in order to gain fresh perspectives. Establish an innovation fund and/or an innovation laboratory that allows people to try new things in a protective and supportive environment.

Walk around and talk to your employees every day, and hear them out. This will encourage them to share their ideas with you in an informal manner. Have a real open-door policy that allows your folks to speak with you in private and to share their ideas, concerns, and proposed solutions. Extensively celebrate creative ideas that have worked, and publically encourage others to submit innovative approaches. Creativity has a momentum of its own; when encouraged, it will flow. When discouraged, it will quickly choke and, ultimately, suffocate.

Promote uniformity and consistency by using the systems we have discussed throughout this book. Develop a mission, a vision, and guiding principles statement that let everyone know what the organization is all about and where it is going. Establish goals and objectives, and share them with everyone so that people know where the organization is going and what it is trying to accomplish. Develop internal manuals and standard operating procedures that explain the organization's policies and procedures. Write organizationwide position descriptions and performance standards that advise everyone what he is supposed to do and how he is supposed to do it.

Each field organization then operates within this framework to ensure there is a common approach toward both doing the work and achieving the goals. Meanwhile, your headquarters/area offices act as checks and balances to ensure that everyone understands that all offices have the same marching orders, are doing business in the same way, and are accomplishing the same things.

By the same token, they should look to find out who has new and exciting ideas, seed these ideas when they have potential, and then share these best practices once they are successful. The key again is to strike a balance between both approaches: to encourage innovation and creativity while also striving for a reasonable degree of uniformity and consistency.

CHAPTER 10

Examples of Improving Performance

It is one thing to understand the principles contained in this book and quite another to successfully apply them. As a result, I am including four examples where I was personally involved in turning around the performance of a government organization.

In the first example, I was a key adviser to a director who was hired to dramatically improve the performance of a claims processing activity. In the second and third examples, I was the director who worked closely with the appropriate division chiefs and their staffs to change the mindset, the systems, the way they managed their operation, and, ultimately, their performance. In the last example, I was on the outside looking in; I was a consultant to a government HRM service that was struggling, and, together, we were able to right the ship and get it moving forward.

As you read these examples, note the following. First, every organization, while facing challenges similar to those faced by the other organizations, was in fact somewhat different from the others I discuss. To me, it brings to mind the opening sentence from *Anna Karenina*, by Leo Tolstoy: "All happy families are alike; each unhappy family is unhappy in its own way." The trick was to identify the systemic problems that were driving the poor performance and then find and implement solutions that would help them in both the short and the long term.

Second, change required a shift in the organization's thought processes. In all cases, there was at the outset a palpable mindset that the organization was virtually unmanageable, and this type of thinking seemed to permeate the organization.

Third, change meant that management was prepared to do what it had to do *as long as it was doing the right thing (even if it was a bit unorthodox) for the right reasons.*

Fourth, it always came down to leadership; the leadership team had to show the way and let people know it was willing to take risks and deal with difficult issues if necessary. Moreover, it had to make it crystal clear to everyone involved that it simply would not accept poor performance.

Let's look at the four examples.

A Claims Processing Activity

This was largest division of an office that was responsible for several business lines. The division itself had approximately 200 employees and was required to process and adjudicate thousands of claims for a variety of different benefits. The division had historically been plagued with a number of problems, including poor performance (especially timeliness of adjudicating claims), limited if any accountability, supervisors who frequently did not understand some of the most important technical components of the work they supervised, poor internal controls, difficult EEO issues, and probably the worst labor relations situation in the entire nation.

More important, the mindset of both the senior leadership team and division management was that their problems were so complex and unique that no one outside the station could appreciate what they were dealing with. In essence, they felt that if their headquarters would acknowledge how difficult their challenges were and simply leave them alone to try to cope, things would somehow be okay. In retrospect, this was a classic case of an organization looking to blame someone else for its problems and sticking its head in the sand and hoping its problems would go away, which of course they didn't.

Eventually, our headquarters encouraged the leader to retire, which he did, and a new director was appointed who refused to accept the excuses of the past. He made it clear to everyone that this was a new era and that there was no reason why our office could not successfully compete with every other one. The person in charge of our claims processing division realized that he was no longer a good fit, so he retired shortly after the arrival of our new director.

Meanwhile, the new director embarked on a series of initiatives intended to make our organization more flexible and better able to respond to workload fluctuations, but they were not particularly well received by some of the troops. For example, he started detailing people from other divisions to our claims processing division in order to reduce some of the pressing backlogs. The other divisions objected, but he didn't buy it and pointed out that we were all in this together and they should stop focusing exclusively on their own silos.

He noted that many of our section chiefs had no experience in rating claims, even though this was one of the most important components of claims processing. He therefore set up a rotation schedule according to which these supervisors were detailed to our rating board so that they could become familiar with the technical components of the job.

Many of the supervisors were outraged by this, feeling that they were going to be exiled to the board and never return to supervision. It was clearly an emotional reaction on their part, driven by their concern that the new director wanted to clean house. However, he gave them the chance to state their case, stood his ground, and then assured them that this was not his intention, and they grudgingly complied. Eventually, they saw the wisdom of this approach as they learned a great deal more about the technical side of the operation and became better supervisors as a result.

The new director was also troubled by the fact that our entire rating board, which had about sixteen people at the time, was all white. He felt, as the station EEO Officer,[1] that it was his responsibility to integrate the board and make it more reflective of our local community. By the same token, he was aware that the internal pool of candidates from which future rating specialists would be chosen was also white. He therefore decided to expand the area of consideration in our vacancy announcements and also consider outside applicants. His rationale was that we would be more likely to reach minority candidates this way while still considering our own employees.

This caused a minor rebellion by some of the white employees, who accused the director of reverse discrimination. In response, the director met with the unhappy employees and patiently listened to their concerns. He then replied that it was hardly reverse discrimination to add one minority employee to a group that had historically been all white. Moreover, he emphasized that it was his legal responsibility to ensure that there was equal opportunity for all and that he had no intention of backing off. Most of the people in the room quickly recognized he was right and dropped the issue. The leader of the "cause" did not accept his explanation and continued to press the matter, but it was clear to everyone else she had lost the argument, and she became further and further isolated after that.

To complicate matters even further, our office had what was widely recognized to be the worst labor relations climate in the nation. We were at war with our local union.

There were days when we received more than a dozen complaints and years where we received more than a hundred Unfair Labor Practice charges (ULPs) and a hundred grievances, this in an organization of fewer than four hundred people! Imagine how difficult this made our lives when we were also trying to cope with a difficult work situation, poor performance, and frequent scrutiny and criticism from our headquarters.

Our initial plan was to try to contain the complaints by training the supervisors on labor relations and trying to build a good relationship with the union, especially the individual filing most of the complaints. While this paid some dividends, the sheer volume of complaints that continued to flow threatened to overwhelm us.

We attempted to simply deal with the complaints in HRM so that the supervisors would not be constantly distracted from their day-to-day work. This definitely helped for a while, but once the supervisors began having to respond to complaints working their way through the system, answer interrogatories from investigators, and testify at arbitrations, we realized that this was not going to solve the problem either. Moreover, as you can imagine, the new director was not very happy with our labor relations program, as he could see that it was making a difficult situation even harder to manage.

We therefore decided to take a different approach to improve the situation. Anytime a complaint was filed in which we believed we were in the wrong, we immediately settled the case. However, when we felt we were in the right, we fiercely contested the complaint, preferring to go to litigation rather than settle and send a message that we were going to cave in every time the union complained.

We also began pushing back at the union; we started filing grievances or ULPs whenever we believed it was in violation of the law or its contract. This put the union on the defensive more than it was used to. Moreover, it made the bargaining unit question why their elected officials were constantly battling management and why they were frequently spending their union dues on arbitrations.

In the middle of all this, a new division chief arrived, and he decided that the division did not have enough controls in place. In addition, he was also troubled by the fact that there were very few internal policy statements available. Finally, he concluded that the employees had not received enough technical training to do their jobs correctly.

He quickly established a plan to address all three of these issues. For example, he set up a system by which pending claims were reviewed more quickly and frequently, so the employees could take appropriate action on a timely basis during each phase of the claims process. He devoted a lot of his time to writing policy memos, so everyone knew what his policies were and how to handle a wide variety of complex situations. Finally, he instituted a comprehensive division-wide training program that ensured that the employees received frequent training on the most important parts of their job.

He also concluded that he had a large number of employees who were not pulling their weight and that action had to be taken on each of them. Since I was the acknowledged expert on HRM issues, he came to me for assistance on how to proceed. I asked him to prepare a list of all the problem employees and explain where each of them was failing; then, together, we would develop a strategy for dealing with them.

The next day, he brought me a list that contained twenty-nine names, yes, twenty-nine problem employees, situations that had to be addressed individually. He made it clear to me that there was no way that his division could achieve its goals unless he either changed the people or *changed the people.*

Recognizing that he was clearly right and that it was the right thing to do, we sat down and carved out a strategy for dealing with all twenty-nine. In some cases, the approach was simply to informally counsel them and let them know that they needed to improve. In other cases, a more formal approach was required, ranging from taking a disciplinary or adverse action, to issuing a leave restriction letter, to giving the employee a performance improvement plan. The bottom line is that, two years later, twenty-three of the employees had left, because they were fired, pushed out the door, or simply chose to leave. The remaining six employees became fully acceptable. The division chief had accomplished what he had set out to do; he had gotten rid of the deadweight and had sent a powerful message that poor performance or behavior was not going to be tolerated.

The new director and division chief stayed for only a few years before moving on to other challenges. However, by the time they left, our office went from meeting virtually no timeliness goals to meeting all thirteen of the goals. Quality and productivity also improved, as did our labor relations climate, and a survey by our headquarters brought a great deal of praise for our office and these two outstanding leaders.

A Vocational Rehabilitation and Employment (VR&E) Division

A VR&E Division is responsible for helping a select group of clients who have an employment impairment to either find a job or live independently, meaning that they had become capable of caring for themselves and living in an independent manner. Most of the focus is normally on the employment side; in order to help clients find employment, the division may send them to a trade school, college, or some other education program; help them set up a small business; or, if the client is job ready, help them write a resume, prepare for an interview, and find a job.

This is a very rewarding area to work in because the employees have direct contact with their customers and can see the impact of their work. At the time, it was nationally mandated that the division be broken up into several components: (1) the division leader and her assistant; (2) a clerical staff who were responsible for setting up most of the paperwork, answering phone calls, and similar tasks; (3) counseling psychologists (CPs), whose job was to evaluate their clients and determine

what the proper course of action was; and (4) vocational rehabilitation specialists (VRSs), whose job was to implement the
rehabilitation plan, track their client's progress, and help them
find a job.

I became the director of a government office that had VR&
E as one of its business lines. The division employed about sixteen employees and was housed in space that was functional
but nondescript. At any one time, we generally served between
one thousand and two thousand clients who were in varying
stages of the rehabilitation process (e.g., application pending,
being assessed, going through an education program, seeking
employment).

I knew the division had a relatively weak reputation, since
the general perception was that it was poorly run and had a
workforce that was below par. However, the one statistic that
really struck me was the number of clients it had rehabilitated
the past year—forty-six. That's right, forty-six. This means that
the entire division rehabilitated three clients for every employee
working there! My first reaction was that maybe we should fire
the entire staff and simply spread their salaries among our clients who were looking for jobs.

Of course, I didn't really mean that, but I actually made that
statement to the division chief and her assistant for illustration
purposes. I wanted her to see how other people were viewing
their division's performance and to let the two of them know I
was very confident that together we could improve their results
by leaps and bounds.

The way I saw things, there were several problems that
needed to be addressed. They were these: (1) The division chief
had lost her confidence because she had been beaten to a pulp
by previous leaders of our organization; (2) some people were

not pulling their weight; (3) the employees did not own the process; (4) the workforce felt little connection to the mission and believed it was neglected by the organization; (5) the physical plant sent a message to the employees that neither their customers nor their performance was important; and (6) no one was really focused on the bottom line—rehabilitating our clients.

Here is what we did to address each one of these problems. With respect to the division chief, we quickly concluded she was a smart and dedicated individual who simply needed someone to support her and show her a better way to get the job done. We taught her about total quality management, visual management, and systems thinking and explained to her how to effectively handle a variety of personnel situations. We gave her books to read and introduced her to other successful leaders, and she started to take a series of steps that let us know she was going to not only make it but blossom.

She began to realize there was more than one way to do things, and she didn't have to manage by blaming others. In essence, this was the way she had been taught or at least what she thought she had learned by watching some of her previous bosses operate. As the fog lifted and she learned to manage in a better way, she slowly but surely came out of her shell and emerged as a dynamic and respected leader.

She also learned the value of dealing with poor performers, which was important since she had several problem employees. She began to see that if you don't deal with poor performers, others will take the message that your organization is not serious about high performance, and things will inevitably start to slide.

Eventually, this division chief did take action against several of her worst employees, and, lo and behold, they left the organization. I'll never forget seeing her expression the first time she was able to get rid of one of her longtime problems. She told me that she never thought she could pull that off and that it was not nearly as difficult as she had been led to believe.

From that moment on, she became more confident in her abilities and more determined to deal with employees who were not pulling their weight. More important, everyone else got the same message, and the division's performance began to steadily climb.

Meanwhile, the importance of having one of her problem employees leave was hammered home even further when she started to dole out his pending work to other employees. She was shocked to discover he had been sitting on a lot of unfinished work that had been pending for months and months without action. This employee's performance had truly been a disaster, and she vowed never to let that happen again.

Concerning the employees' not owning the process, a major problem was that no one was held accountable for whether or not her clients were rehabilitated. In other words, the number of clients rehabilitated was nowhere to be found in anyone's performance standards, meaning that, for all intents and purposes, no one took ownership of the results.

We took action to place this metric in both the division chief's and in her assistant's performance standards and also wanted to include it in the standards of the CPs and VRSs. However, she resisted including it in those employees' standards for two reasons: (1) They were "professionals" and shouldn't be treated that way; and (2) since the CPs handed the work off to the VRSs, neither of them should be held accountable for the number of clients rehabilitated.

Eventually, she realized that professionals had to play by the same set of rules as everyone else. That is, there was absolutely no reason why they should not be held to a set of measurable standards like every other member of the organization. Once she saw the wisdom of this approach, she quickly bought into it.

She had a harder time accepting the argument that both the CPs and the VRSs should have a standard involving the number of veterans rehabilitated. We kept emphasizing that these two positions worked together as a team toward the rehabilitation of a defined group of customers, so it was natural they should share the standard, but she resisted, feeling she could never sell it to the employees. We finally responded by posing this question: What design choice would best ensure that the two positions would work together to help clients get jobs? After thinking it over, she finally agreed that a joint standard would encourage the right behavior, but she was still concerned about what the reaction would be from the troops.

She distributed the standard for comment and was surprised to find that the employees were generally supportive of the concept and were willing to give it a try. She gave it out, people quickly got used to it, it never became a problem, and it certainly drove the right behavior.

Regarding the employees' feeling that they were neglected by the organization, there was definitely some truth to that perception. The division was the smallest business line on station and the one that generally received the least attention for two primary reasons: (1) most of the national focus was on claims processing because that was the area that was constantly in the news; and (2) its work processes and legal requirements were relatively technical and not well understood by most senior leaders, who generally gave them little more than lip service.

In order to address this issue, either my assistant or I made sure we visited the division every day, said "hello" to the employees, tried to learn what was on their minds, and answered any questions they had. We also held periodic meetings with them (either monthly or quarterly, depending on circumstances), during which we briefed them about how things were going with respect to both their division and the station, explained what the current issues and concerns were at the national level, and gave them the chance to ask anything they wanted to. Over time, this effort bought us a lot of credibility with the division's employees and brought them back into the fold of the overall organization.

With respect to the physical plant, in my opinion it was neutral at best; the space was okay from both an aesthetic and a functional perspective. However, if okay is what you are looking for, that is all you will get. We wanted to provide the employees with a physical plant they could be proud of and one that sent a message that our customers, our employees, and, most important, performance were all important.

As a result, we hung banners from the ceiling that reminded both the employees and visitors that finding our customers jobs was our top priority. Next to the banners we hung pictures of our clients to remind everyone that they were the reason why we were in business. We also set up a bulletin board that told some of our success stories and included with each a photograph of our employee with a satisfied customer. Finally, we converted the division's conference room into a war room in which we displayed all of the division's key performance indicators and trend data. In this way, employees were better able to use data when making key decisions, and they started to see the bigger picture, understand the importance of performance, and see the same information that previously only management had been privy to.

As stated earlier, the last and perhaps the greatest concern we had was that no one was concerned about the bottom line, which was rehabilitating our clients. By this we meant either finding them jobs or getting them to the point where they could live independently. In order to address this issue, every time I saw the division chief and/or her assistant, the first thing I asked was, "How many rehabs have you had so far this month?"

After a while, it became well known around the station that this was always going to be my first question, and it became something of a running joke. In fact, she used to say that I would first ask her about the number of rehabs and then how she was doing. However, the point was made, and, within a short period of time, she became much more focused on the bottom line and effectively communicated this message to her employees.

The number of clients rehabilitated per year steadily increased from forty-six to sixty-nine to more than 100 and eventually exceeded 400. Along these lines, I fondly recall one staff meeting when the division chief proudly announced they had rehabilitated forty-six clients for that month—the same number that they had previously rehabilitated in an entire year!

What a great feeling to see someone who at one time had been battered, bruised, and bad-mouthed grow into a proud and confident leader. The corollary to the story is that, down the road, when Congress held a hearing on how to improve the VR&E Program, she was the only VR&E officer who was asked to testify. Now that's improvement!

A Home Loan Guaranty Program

Our home loan guaranty program was responsible for helping our clients get home mortgages at low rates and with little money down by guaranteeing 25 percent of the loan amount. In the event our customers failed to repay their loans on time, we would service the loan and try and develop a plan for how they would become current. If that didn't work and they defaulted on the loan, we would further attempt to assist them by trying to find alternatives to foreclosure. If all else failed, we would often purchase the property from the lender and then try to sell it ourselves. As you can imagine, a lot of people were affected by this program, and a lot of money was at stake.

The division employed more than 130 people and served a catchment area of 1.2 million potential clients. At the time I took over, it owned roughly three thousand foreclosed properties.

This division had the well-earned reputation of being the worst loan guaranty division in the nation. Timeliness was poor, accuracy was low, productivity was abysmal, and customers did not like doing business with it. Moreover, it had by far the worst filing system I had ever seen; files were sitting all over the place, and the system was out of control. To make matters even worse, the division had low morale and little or no accountability, but it did have several angry and discontented employees, some of whom were also poor performers, who were loud and distracting and who were clearly pulling the division down. Finally, the division had several employees who were frequent EEO filers, people who tended to see everything in terms of race and who were not shy about filing EEO complaints if they were dissatisfied with a management decision and/or to do so would suit their purpose at the time. Otherwise, things were going quite well, thank you.

We decided to immediately focus on the filing system, which was in atrocious shape, to put things mildly. Files were piled higher than an elephant's eye, in no particular order, in rows and rows of dreary government space. Since the file clerks rarely were able to get their hands on folders they were searching for, our technicians often created "dummy files" in order to get the work done. I was told that we often had four or five dummy folders per client.

We concluded that, given the size and scope of our files, we did not have the capacity to quickly resolve the problems with the resources we had on hand. After all, we were being inundated with work, and we had to continue to try to serve our customers. We therefore decided to hire a temporary employment firm to come in and quickly turn the files around. We took this approach because we could bring the temps on quickly and because they had the both the ability and the capacity to address the situation on hand.

Within a month, the files were completely revamped, and we had some semblance of order. I say "some" because so much damage had occurred from many years of neglect that the best we could do was bring order to the mess and try to go forward from there with a system that would serve us well in the future. The good news was that our rate of finding files immediately increased from the 20–30 percent range to between 70 percent and 80 percent, which was a big improvement, although certainly not what we were looking for in the long term.

As an aside, a memorable story emerged out of this initiative when a temporary worker found a piece of paper that had been sitting under one of the file cabinets. It turned out to be a loan request that had been pinned under the cabinet for more than ten years! I immediately seized upon this as a symbol of our past failures and had the document framed and prominently hung it on a wall in the division. The point here was to let everyone know that we were fully aware of how bad our service had been in the past and that we were determined to never let it happen again.

Eventually, we purchased a brand-new set of rotating file cabinets that were safe, secure, and efficient and that made it easy to retrieve files. This purchase, coupled with tighter controls and a new files supervisor, ensured that we continued to improve the management of our filing system.

After making progress with our filing system, our division chief retired, and his assistant stepped down. Until we could find a new team, I made my assistant the acting division chief. We then put a lot of time and effort into recruiting people who we thought would be good fits for the division management team, and we wound up finding an excellent division chief and assistant. They were strong, dedicated people who were willing to learn, were prepared to deal with difficult issues, and wanted to make a difference. We were confident these were the right individuals to help us make a quantum leap forward.

Once they were in place, they immediately laid the groundwork to make the division function as intended. They put in place standard operating procedures, placed a high degree of importance on tracking data, developed better performance standards, began to conduct random samples to test the quality of each employee's work, and made it clear to everyone they would not tolerate poor performance or misconduct. The fact they were willing to deal head-on with some long-standing personnel issues made me confident we were going to be okay.

For example, one of our sections had several employees who were always complaining and seemed to spend more time keeping a log of what our supervisors were saying and doing than they spent serving our customers. At one point, the assistant division chief came to us and told us that, because of the impact of those employees, their section would be able to achieve its goals only if we gave them more FTE employees. We told him we didn't have any FTE to give him but that we would help him deal with these two problem employees. Within six months, he got rid of both of them, and, despite not receiving any additional FTE to replace them, the section wound up meeting all of its goals. It learned a valuable lesson that sometimes you can have addition by subtraction.

Meanwhile, the division chief and his assistant were also open to new ideas, and together we found innovative ways to do our work that made us more effective, efficient, and customer friendly. For instance, they were concerned about the process we followed to advertise our properties, select the successful bidders, and then notify each bidder. At that time, we (as well as all other divisions around the country that had the same mission) would advertise our properties in the newspaper, have our employees manually review all of the bids, decide who the winning bidders were, and then write letters to all parties notifying them of our decisions.

From our perspective, there were multiple problems with this process. First of all, it was very expensive. For example, we were paying roughly $80,000 per month to place full-page advertisements for our properties in the newspaper. Second, two or three full-time employees were required to review the bids, decide who the winning bidders were, and so on. All told, it was a costly, expensive, and inefficient process.

The solution was to advertise all of our properties on the Internet and have all of the people who wished to purchase our properties submit electronic bids. Since the bids were electronic, we simply programmed our computer system to make the requisite calculations, decide who the winning bidders were, and send the decision letters to everyone.

The net result of this initiative was to save the office roughly $1 million per year and to enable the two or three FTE who used to work on the bidding process to perform other tasks. Moreover, our customers were thrilled, as they received faster and better service from our office. Finally, other offices adopted this initiative, which wound up saving the national organization roughly $12 million per year and freed up dozens of FTE.

The bottom line here was that we worked closely with the new chief and his assistant, and they brought a degree of order, discipline, professionalism, and a willingness to think outside the box. They let everyone know that high performance was expected, set up a solid set of management systems, implemented them effectively, were willing to deal with difficult issues, and encouraged creativity. The division, which was once considered to be the worst out of forty-six in the nation, wound up being ranked as the number one division on the national organization's balanced scorecard. Whereas at one point it had roughly three thousand properties in its inventory, that total eventually declined to fewer than 100.

A Human Resources Management (HRM) Service

An HRM service is responsible for providing a full range of services to its parent organization, which in this case was a medical center. Among the services it was tasked with providing were staffing, position classification, employee and labor relations, training and development, processing and records, incentive awards, workers' compensation, and employee benefits and programs (e.g., transit vouchers, leave donations).

The health care system that HRM serviced is one of the largest and most complex health care systems in government, employing roughly five thousand people, many of whom are out-based as far as ninety miles from the main hub. Its HRM service is believed to be the largest field operation in the national organization, employing close to ninety FTE.

The health care system has historically had problems with the performance of its HRM service. Customers have constantly complained about the service they received. In addition, performance indicators (the few they had) also showed that performance was poor; the service had difficulty in both filling jobs on a timely basis and dealing with difficult employees; it has had frequent turnover, including at the management level; morale was low; and the physical plant was abysmal.

As sort of a last-ditch effort, senior management hired me as a consultant to assess the system's operation and make recommendations to improve it. I interviewed a wide variety of HRM service employees, as well as many of its customers and stakeholders. I also reviewed dozens of different documents (e.g., audits and surveys of HRM, internal studies) that provided me with a full and fair picture of its strengths and weaknesses. I paid particular attention to the impact that HRM was having on the health care system's ability to meet its mission (e.g., I reviewed its mission performance metrics as shown on the Intranet, performance evaluations of the system, and the director's performance standards), and I attended the director's staff meetings. In approaching this project, I used the OSD model as a guide for examining HRM in a systematic manner and looking at the way each system and design choice related to the others.

I then provided a full and fair assessment of the structure, assessed the management skill sets and effectiveness, and provided a series of recommendations on how to improve the activity. The client was very pleased with the report and subsequently contracted with me to implement it.

One of my tasks was to develop the management staff, so I mentored the acting personnel officer for at least an hour a day and the other supervisors at least once a week. The acting personnel officer responded very well to our mentoring sessions and tried to soak up as much knowledge as possible. Several of the other supervisors were just as enthusiastic, and they too developed very quickly.

Since timeliness of service was such a big issue with HRM's customers, we began by designing performance tracking systems from the perspective of their customers. This was particularly important because, in some cases, it seemed as though HRM employees and their customers were not on the same page.

For example, when it came to tracking the time it took HRM to process certain actions, the service started the clock when it received all the evidence necessary to process an action. By using this approach, in most cases, on paper it was processing actions in fewer than ten days. The problem was that customers were telling me that, in many cases, HRM was taking months to process their actions.

HRM then started tracking each action from the first day one of its customers contacted the office, not from the day it received all of the requested evidence. Once it did this, it found that the average processing time rose to seventy-one days! Obviously, this was not solely a reflection of how long HRM was taking to process the claims actions, but it did let managers know more precisely why their clients were frustrated. It also enabled them to better explain to senior management why actions were taking so long—that more than 80 percent of the delay was due to clients' behavior, not their actions. Moreover, they started to track the reasons why all of the information was not being properly submitted, and this placed them in a better position to train their customers on how to submit the right information the first time.

In the area of recruitment and placement, HRM decided to track not only how long the entire process took but also each component of the process (e.g., time from the submission of a Standard Form 52, Request for Personnel Action, to the station's Position Management Committee to final approval, the time from approval to classifying the position, and so on). In this way, they could isolate gaps in the process and more easily find ways to resolve them.

Along these lines, we worked to redesign all of the service's performance standards in order to build more accountability into the system. Up to that point, the standards were very vague and made it very difficult for management to hold the employees accountable. Now, where possible, HRM started tracking each employee's performance in the areas of output, accuracy, timeliness, and customer satisfaction. It was able to capture some of this information from our new tracking systems, although we had to add two additional tracking mechanisms.

First, it developed monthly statistical quality control sheets for its key positions. In this way, the supervisors could randomly and methodically track the quality of each employee's work. Very quickly, patterns began to emerge, and, for the first time, several of the supervisors started to see some performance deficiencies they had not previously been aware of. This prompted discussions with some of the employees on how to improve their accuracy, which in my view was definitely a good thing.

With respect to customer satisfaction, HRM started a program through which it surveyed its clients twice a year on how well each of their employees was serving them. This sent a powerful message to both the employees and their clients that HRM was now serious about delivering quality service.

To reinforce the importance of performance, HRM purchased a series of bulletin boards for both the service and each of its sections. It used the boards to share performance information with every employee, solicit their ideas as to how the organization could improve its performance, and let them know that management would be looking at its indicators more closely than ever. These bulletin boards also sent a strong message to HRM's customers that the service was committed to excellence and was not the HRM service of the past.

We also provided the management team with guidance and training on how to deal with a number of difficult personnel issues and met with its regional counsel in order to influence its approach to representing the health care system. In my view, if both HRM and, by extension, the entire health care system were able to build true accountability into their organization, they would make a quantum leap forward. The point here was to reinforce the importance of dealing with difficult people, rather than simply moving them around, as most government organizations seem to do.

The physical plant was one of the worst I have ever seen in government, and that is saying a lot, since I have seen some pretty dismal work areas in my time. First of all, the space was not functional. The building's configuration reminded me of a submarine, with people cramped into very tight quarters. In addition, the sections were organized in an illogical manner, meaning the wrong sections were situated next to each other. For example, Position Classification should sit next to Staffing, yet they were on opposite sides of the floor. Moreover, in many cases, the supervisors were located away from the employees they were supervising.

The building also had virtually no security, and there were several unlocked doors where visitors could enter. In fact, on several occasions, homeless people were seen giving themselves sponge baths in the employees' restrooms.

Finally, the space was very unattractive and unappealing. The walls were painted in dull colors, which tended to make the lighting seem even worse than it already was. A series of nondescript, boring pictures lined the hallways, and there was no employee recognition visible. It was even hard to tell what the mission of the organization was, since little evidence of it adorned the walls.

To address all of these physical plant issues, HRM put together a comprehensive space redesign plan. The first thing was to redo the work flow so that the essential contingencies were preserved. For example, this meant placing Classification on one side of Staffing and Processing and Records on the other side. HRM also ensured that all of the supervisors were situated next to or near their subordinates. Finally, where possible, it tried to knock down non-load-bearing walls in order to open up the space a bit and give the employees more breathing room.

Concerning the security issue, HRM locked the side doors from the outside (the employees were provided keys) and funneled all visitors through the front entrance. Beyond a certain point, an HRM employee had to buzz nonemployees through a locked door in order to enter the main hub.

It also developed a new color scheme that entailed adding some sharp accents to the current scheme. The idea here was that accents would offer a contrast and make the space appear to be a bit brighter and more alive. HRM then acquired a series of photographs that were more reflective of the mission and proudly displayed them in the hallways. These were very well received by all concerned. Finally, HRM made plans to take photographs of each section's employees and hang these photographs outside each section along with each section's performance metrics.

By the time my assignment had been completed, the redesign of the physical plant had been set in motion, but every element had not yet been implemented due to cost factors and other priorities within the health care system. However, all of the plans were expected to be implemented within the next fiscal year at the latest, and together they will help contribute to the transformation of the HRM service.

The results of their efforts quickly became apparent. For example, performance improved in virtually all areas once HRM developed a good system for tracking performance, was able to identify gaps, and put into place effective countermeasures. The percentage of positions classified within ten days increased from 93 percent to 100 percent. The percentage of retention incentives processed within ten days rose from 0 percent to more than 61 percent. The processing of administrative requests for personnel actions on a timely basis increased from

56 percent to 96 percent, and the accuracy of these actions increased from 83 percent to 100 percent. Also, in one month, the time it took to process a disciplinary or adverse action improved by 23 percent *from the customer's perspective*. Finally, an internal customer survey and anecdotal data both revealed that satisfaction with HRM had clearly improved.

As you can, in these four situations the performance improvement effort had to be adapted at least somewhat to the circumstances (the activity's mission and vision, the skill and attitude of the management team, the quality and experience levels of the workforce, the organization's culture, its management systems, its ability to deal with difficult people, its physical plant). However, the approach was always the same: analyze the situation by talking to the managers, employees, customers, and/or stakeholders; review the applicable data, reports, and information; and then identify the performance gaps. From there, we focused on four primary areas: (1) developing managers and employees; (2) improving and aligning the systems; (3) successfully implementing the improvements in a clear and consistent manner; and (4) encouraging innovation and creativity.

Such an approach allowed me to look at everything on a holistic basis and to understand the cause and effect of each design choice. The key here was not only to make a quick fix but also to make changes that would last for the long term. It was not rocket science, but it did take a lot of looking, listening, and analyzing and then making sure that we went forward with a comprehensive and integrated plan that was designed to address the root causes of each organization's problems.

You, too, can do it. All you need is the will and the skill.

Notes

Chapter 1

1. For further information, see the Office of Management and Budget's website on this subject: http://www.whitehouse.gov/omb/mgmt-gpra_gplaw2m/, accessed July 31, 2009.

2. "GPRA," by Strategisy, LLC, http://www.john-mercer.com/gpra.htm, accessed August 3, 2009.

3. GPRA, Section (b).

4. The backlog exceeded a million cases if you count pending ratings, nonrating work, appeals, etc.

5. The federal government defines an adverse action as a removal, suspension of more than fourteen days, or a change to lower grade. A disciplinary action would refer to a suspension of fourteen days or less or a less punitive action such as an admonishment or reprimand.

6. See "Defense Base Closure and Realignment Commission, Final Report to the President," September 8, 2005, http://www.brac.gov/docs/final/Volume1BRACReport.pdf.

7. There are many different unions that represent government employees. They range from the American Federation of Government Employees (AFGE) to the National Treasury Employees Unions (NTEU) to the American Federation of State, County and Municipal Employees (AFSCME). Depending upon the circumstances, more than one union can represent the employees of a specific government organization.

8. For one perspective, see "Pay for Performance Shares Problems Between Federal Employees and Contractors," July 6, 2009, by Mark Gibson, Labor Relations Specialist, Washington, D.C., Unionblog.com, http://www.afge.org/Index.cfm? Page = UnionBlog&FuseAction = View&BlogID = 663, accessed July 31, 2009.

9. This refers to the government employees who came on around the end of the Vietnam War.

10. For a more detailed description of how to manage government employees, see *Managing Government Employees: How to Motivate Them, Deal with Difficult Issues and Produce Tangible Results,* by Stewart Liff (AMACOM Books, 2007).

11. The one exception being Chapter 7, which addresses both the rewards and recognition and renewal systems.

Chapter 2

1. Shelley E. Phipps, "The System Design Approach to Organizational Development: The University of Arizona Model," *Library Trends,* Summer, 2004.

2. Much of this chapter and the next are based on my years of discussions with Paul, on his *Organizational Systems Design Guidebook* (OPD, Inc. 1996), and on the *Five Smooth Stones: Guidebook* (San Jose, CA), and *Organization Planning and Design,* by Gustavson and Alyson S. Von Feldt (2009).

3. Office of Management and Budget, "Primer on Performance Measurement" (revised February 28, 1995), http://govinfo.library.unt.edu/npr/library/resource/gpraprmr.html, accessed September 29, 2009.

4. I will discuss both of these approaches in more detail under the chapter that deals with the decision-making and information systems.

5. Social Security Online, www. socialsecurity.gov, http://www .ssa.gov/aboutus/, accessed October 1, 2009.

6. Official website of the Los Angeles Police Department, http:// www.lapdonline.org/inside_the_lapd/content_basic_view/ 844, accessed October 1, 2009.

7. United States Environmental Protection Agency, http://www .epa.gov/progress/#b, accessed October 1, 2009.

8. For more detailed information on visual management, read *Seeing Is Believing: How the New Art of Visual Management Can Boost Performance Throughout Your Organization*, by Stewart Liff and Pamela A. Posey, D.B.A. (AMACOM Books, 2004).

9. Gustavson and Von Feldt, *Five Smooth Stones: Guidebook.*

Chapter 3

1. Gustavson and Von Feldt, *Five Smooth Stones: Guidebook.*

2. The Requirements Solutions Group, LLC, "How to Model, Analyze and Improve Business Processes," http://www.require mentssolutions.com/How_to_Model_Analyze_Improve_Busi ness_Processes.html#, accessed October 4, 2009.

3. Business Dictionary.com, http://www.businessdictionary.- com/definition/business-process-reengineering-BPR.html#, accessed October 5, 2009.

4. A large portion of the history of the reinventing government initiative was gleaned from the document, "National Partner- ship for Reinventing Government (Formerly the National Performance Review), A Brief History," by John Kamensky, January 1999.

5. David Osborne and Ted Gaebler, *Reinventing Government: How the Entrepreneurial Spirit Is Transforming the Public Sec- tor* (The Penguin Group, 1993).

6. Al Gore, "Creating a Government That Works Better and Costs Less, Report of the National Performance Review," Office of the Vice President, September 1994.

7. In writing this history of the New York Regional Office's reengineering efforts, I relied both on my own memory and on James Thompson's excellent article, "Joe versus the Bureaucracy," *Government Executive Magazine*, October 1, 1995.

8. See Gustavson, *Organizational Systems Design Guidebook* (OPD, Inc. 1996) and *Five Smooth Stones: Guidebook*.

9. A PMC is responsible for reviewing requests to fill vacant positions and determining whether it is in the best interests of the organization to fill that position.

10. For more information on people's learning preferences, see *The Whole Brain Business Book*, by Ned Hermann (McGraw-Hill, 1996).

11. For example, GSA's "First Impressions Program" strives to improve major lobby and plaza spaces in and around federal buildings. U.S. General Services Administration, "Improve Your Space," http://www.gsa.gov/Portal/gsa/ep/contentView.do?contentType = GSA_BASIC&contentId = 24585&noc = T, accessed October 21, 2009.

12. The dress code banned jeans, tee shirts, sneakers, baseball caps, etc., which were commonly worn by our employees up to then.

Chapter 4

1. Minnesota Department of Health, "Organization Design Principles," http://www.health.state.mn.us/about/strategic/orgprinciples.html, dated September 12, 2006.

2. By an overall structure, I am referring to an entire government institution that is national, statewide, or local in scope.

3. For example, a contractor took over the VA's property management program and did such a bad job that their contract was quickly cancelled.

4. As recommended by the National Performance Review.

5. National Partnership for Reinventing Government, "Transforming Organizational Structure," http://govinfo.library.unt .edu/npr/library/reports/tosexe.html, accessed November 9, 2009.

6. It is important to understand that the government has many dedicated and excellent clerks. I am simply stating that based on my experience, they tend to both have and cause more problems than higher-graded and skilled workers.

7. Everyone can't do direct labor because you need some degree of supervisory and support overhead. The key is to have the right amount, and not too much. Moreover, you should not have poor employees sitting around in "make work" jobs because management simply does not want to deal with them.

Chapter 5

1. The Health Insurance Portability and Accountability Act of 1996.

2. The Federal Information Security Management Act of 2002.

3. Wayne Eckerson, "What Are Performance Dashboards?" *Information Management Magazine*, November 2005.

4. The Balanced Scorecard Institute, http://www.balancedscore card.org, accessed November 23, 2009.

5. By Robert S. Kaplan and David, P. Norton, Harvard Business Press, 1996.

Chapter 6

1. Obviously, you can't plan for every contingency and unanticipated vacancies will most surely occur. However, the wider the number of possible openings that you plan for, the less frequent will be your ad hoc recruitment efforts.

2. More veterans were likely to qualify at the GS-12 level than at the GS-13 level.

3. If filled at the GS-12 level, the veteran could then be promoted after a year to the GS-13 level if her performance was satisfactory.

4. Although currently there are plenty of applicants for virtually every government job due to the economy that will change when the economy improves.

5. In low-cost areas, where housing is cheaper, taxes are lower and commutes are shorter, government jobs tend to be far more desirable because they more than pay the bills and provide a great deal of stability. Conversely, in high-cost areas, most top-notch candidates do not apply for government jobs because the private sector offers them a much more competitive salary.

Chapter 7

1. I'm not going to spend much time on managing employee behavior as that is covered extensively in my books *Managing Government Employees: How to Motivate Them, Deal with Difficult Issues and Produce Tangible Results* (AMACOM Books, 2007) and *The Complete Guide to Hiring and Firing Government Employees* (AMACOM Books, 2009).

2. Title 5—Administrative Personnel, Chapter I—Office of Personnel Management, Part 430 Perfromance Management—Table of Contents, Subpart B Performance Appraisal for General Schedule, Prevailing Rate, and Certain Other Employees, Sec. 430.203 Definitions.

3. Conceived by George Lucas, the first film was originally released on May 25, 1977, by 20th Century Fox.

4. In computing productivity, you usually divide an employee's standard output by a denominator, which often represents the number of hours the employee is available on the job. For example, if an employee completed forty standard hours of work in a given week, you might divide that total by forty hours if the employee was at work for the entire week. Thus 40/40 = 100%, which would represent the employee's productivity. However, if the employee is on leave for part of the week, attending training or meetings, and/or working on a special project, you might want to consider excluding some or all of this time from their individual productivity calculation.

5. Three hundred and sixty degree feedback comes from all around an employee. The number "360" stems from the 360 degrees of a circle, with the person appraised being within the circle. Three hundred and sixty feedback is typically provided by peers, supervisors, stakeholders, and subordinates if the person being appraised is a supervisor.

Chapter 8

1. There are other ways of rating people such as "exceptional," "very good," and "satisfactory." The actual terminology depends upon the organization's system.

2. Technically, giving an employee a fully satisfactory rating and/or not giving her an award is not a negative action. However,

over the years, supervisors have given out so many high ratings and awards that many employees tend to view the absence of a high rating and/or an award as being an adverse event. The best way to change this mindset is to have reliable consequences for all levels of performance so that employees recognize that they are not "owed" a high rating and/or an award for average performance; they truly have to earn it.

3. I have also used television monitors to track performance within each team. The upside of this approach is that it is jazzier, more modern, and attractive to the eye. The downside is that it can be expensive to install, may take more time to maintain, and can create computer security issues if it is tied directly into the organization's computer system.

4. *Managing Government Employees: How to Motivate Them, Deal with Difficult Issues and Produce Tangible Results* (AMA-COM Books, 2007) and *The Complete Guide to Hiring and Firing Government Employees* (AMACOM Books, 2009).

5. In this circumstance, I decided that I needed coaches, not a series of traditional supervisors. As a result, we abolished all of the first- and second-level supervisory positions, established coach positions with new position descriptions, and let the former supervisors and all other interested candidates apply. Those former supervisors who were not selected were reassigned to direct labor positions at the same grade level.

Chapter 9

1. Under this approach, a deserving employee receives a lottery card that is then placed in a locked box along with the cards of other recipients. At the end of a fixed period of time, several cards are drawn from the box and some form of rewards (dinner for two, movie tickets, etc.) is then given to the "lottery winners."

2. For example, see Brian Friel, "Seeing Is Believing," *Government Executive Magazine*, July 1, 2002, http://www.govexec.com/features/0702/0702s1s1.htm.

Chapter 10

1. In our organization at that time, every director was also the station's EEO Officer.

Index